A Funny Thing Happened
on the Road Less Traveled

A Funny Thing Happened on the Road Less Traveled

Jeremy Sonnenburg

iUniverse, Inc.

New York Lincoln Shanghai

A Funny Thing Happened on the Road Less Traveled

iUniverse, Inc.

For information address:
iUniverse, Inc.
2021 Pine Lake Road, Suite 100
Lincoln, NE 68512
www.iuniverse.com

Cover designed by Jeremy Sonnenburg
Photographs by Jeremy and Dorothy Sonnenburg

ISBN: 0-595-28182-6

Printed in the United States of America

Dedicated to my loving wife, Dorothy. Thank you for your support, your encouragement, and above all, your patience and good humor during our eight months of travel.

Twenty years from now you will be more disappointed by the things that you didn't do than by the ones you did do. So throw off the bowlines. Sail away from the safe harbor. Catch the trade winds in your sails. Explore. Dream. Discover.

—Mark Twain

Two roads diverged in a woods, and I—I took the one less traveled by, And that has made all the difference.

—Robert Frost

I could not tread these perilous paths in safety, if I did not keep a saving sense of humor.

—Lord Nelson

Contents

Acknowledgements

- To my mother, Professor Ava Zinn of San Jacinto College's English Department. Thank you for your edits, feedback, and assistance during the submission process. I know that as an English teacher you face endless stacks of papers to review. I appreciate you making space on your desk for this project. I could not have done it without you.

- To my good friend Murdo Macmillan. Thank you for your revisions and edits. You are a gifted editor and I was very lucky to have you as part of the team. Your dedication to this project meant a lot to me.

- To my new Katz parents, Dad Katz (Ralph) and Mom Katz (Ellen). Dad Katz, thank you for your detailed review of my book proposal. As always, your business perspective was very insightful. Mom Katz, thank you for your internet research, publication ideas, and encouragement.

- To my stepfather and valued friend, Kenny Zinn. Thank you for your assistance during the submission process. Your role as "Kinko's Liaison and Chief Negotiator" was crucial.

- To my brother, Devin Sonnenburg. Thank you for providing much-needed perspective when I became frustrated with the publication process. Sometimes we get our sights so set on the destination we forget to enjoy the view along the way.

- To Professor Carolyn Poole of San Jacinto College's English Department and Mrs. Patsy Hall of Frendship High School's English Department. Thank you both for helping with editorial reviews.

- To Rika Ikeoka. Thank you for your assistance with the Japanese translations.

- To my new brother Mikie Katz. Thank you for getting the video.

- To my new brother Stuie Katz. Thank you for getting the Sprite.

- Finally, to everyone on the original travel comedy distribution list. Thank you all for your many replies to my first few stories. Without your collective encouragement, I would have never considered writing this book.

Introduction

On September 25, 1997, I showed up for my first day of work as a management consultant. In one hand, I held a leather attaché that I couldn't afford, in the other, a newly-minted college degree. I championed my only designer-label suit, which looked a bit tattered from frequent wear through the interview process, complemented by the standard issue white dress shirt and red tie. My undershirt was drenched from a grueling ride through the Houston morning traffic in my old Jeep with no air-conditioning, but there was no *visible* damage. Equipped with my cell phone and electronic organizer, it was undeniable: I was on my way.

I was soon introduced to the other new hires, all looking equally eager to pursue their quest of the American high-powered corporate career. As I circled the room with the best grip and grin I could manage, I met Dorothy, a loud, assertive New Yorker whom I would eventually marry.

My new colleagues and I spent six weeks together in a blurred frenzy of training, long lunches, and corporate happy hours that ran late into the evenings. We emerged as something of a professional pledge class ready to help our clients streamline processes, reduce costs, increase revenues, stabilize earnings, achieve innovation, build knowledge capital, develop strategies, appease stakeholders, leverage technology, and take over the world.

At that time, Dorothy and I were in serious relationships with other people. So, we started off as just friends. Time passed, and so did our other relationships. Two years later, I caught her stealing glances over the water cooler and lingering too long on the occasional hug. I knew it was time to make my move. I turned on the old Don Juan charm, she couldn't resist, and our relationship soon took a romantic turn.

Later that year, on a lazy Sunday afternoon, Dorothy and I were strolling around the University of Texas campus enjoying the sunny Austin weather. As I recounted my glory days as a college student and Dorothy listened in tolerant amusement, we soon found ourselves seeking shelter from the hot Texas sun in the café of a local campus bookstore. With air conditioning blowing down and cold beverages in hand, we continued reminiscing and meandered our way into the "What do you really want to do with your life?" conversation. Two and a half years of seventy-hour workweeks had taken its toll on our professional aspirations, and we both readily agreed there was more to life than successful careers. We discussed a shared longing for adventure, excitement, new challenges, and the thrill of faraway lands. The more we talked, the more passionate we became. Finally, we made a pact. We would work hard for three more years, save diligently, and use the money to take a trip around the world. We did some rough calculations on the back of a napkin to determine the cost of such a trip and created a savings plan. The following Monday, we opened a joint account and started putting away money for our dream. At that moment, I knew she was the woman I wanted to spend the rest of my life with.

About a year later, I decided it was time to pop the big question. Being a proper Texas gentleman, I decided to ask Dorothy's parents for permission before I actually proposed. While I was home visiting my family for the Christmas holidays, I called Dorothy's father, Ralph, and asked to sit down with him and Dorothy's mother, Ellen, in New York the following week. I emphasized that I didn't want Dorothy to be present at this conversation or even to be aware that we were planning it. He played it cool and said he would figure something out, but I have a sneaking suspicion he knew what was coming. Well, sort of.

A couple of days later I flew to New York to join Dorothy and her family for holiday festivities. That evening, while my better half was curled up reading in her bedroom, I snuck into the study and asked Ralph if he had figured out when we were going to have our little chat. He said he hadn't come up with a plan because he couldn't think of a way to divert Dorothy's attention.

Being a clever guy with a flair for the dramatic, I proposed the following: "Halfway through dinner this evening, I'll pretend I'm feeling ill. Dorothy will take notice and ask if I'm OK. I'll give the gab about how I'm not feeling well, and say that perhaps it was something I ate. She'll then ask what she can do for me, and I'll request that she run to the video store to rent a movie while I go lie down and try to recover. That will leave us enough time to have our chat." Ralph loved it. He gave me a high five, and I left the room thinking I was the craftiest man alive.

Later that evening, it was "go" time. Now, my mother was a drama teacher, and I was in theatre classes before I could walk, so when I decide to lay it on, you get a quality performance. I went silent, my face pale, my eyes beady, and I sporadically winced with pain. My palms were clammy and my lower lip was slightly quivering. Dorothy was right on cue. "Jeremy, are you OK?"

"Actually, babe, I'm not feeling so hot. Must be something I ate. That last pork dumpling tasted a bit funny. I don't know why, but I feel terrible." This was going great. I deserved an Oscar.

"Is there anything I can do to help you?" Bingo. I couldn't have scripted it any better. Ralph and I were both wondering if I shouldn't take up a career as an actor.

I didn't miss a beat. "Well, babe, I'd really like to just lie down for a while. Do you mind driving to the video store to rent a movie for me? I've been wanting to see *Gladiator*." Nice! I was going to get her parents' blessing and get to watch one of the best guy flicks of all time in the same evening.

"Sure, honey, no problem."

Perfect. Even with my great acting skills, I had to work hard to contain my smile. Thirty minutes later we were back at the house. Then, the first bomb dropped. "Jer, honey, I've been thinking about it, and I don't think I should leave you here alone while I go and get a movie. MIKIE, GET DOWN HERE!" Her twenty-one-year-old brother Michael came pounding down the stairs. "Jeremy is not feeling well, and I want you to go get him a movie."

"But I was planning to meet my friends in ten minutes to go hang out," he protested.

"Mikie, Jeremy is very sick and I want you to go get him a movie now!" Mikie hung his head in defeat, grabbed the car keys and was out the door before I could absorb what had just happened.

Now I really was starting to feel a little sick to my stomach. She had just unraveled the efforts of one of the better theatrical performances of the century. I knew I had to think fast. What to do, what to do? I took a punt.

"Babe, do you have any Sprite? It helps to settle my stomach."

Frown. "Let me check. Ah, we're in luck; we have 7-Up."

I knew I was pushing it. "Oh, babe, it has to be Sprite. 7-Up won't work."

I could hear the edge creeping into her voice. "Jeremy, it's the same stuff. I'm sure it'll work fine."

I have always believed that persistency pays. "No, babe, it *has* to be Sprite. I don't want to trouble you, so if you don't want to drive to the store, I can just walk." That should do it. She would definitely go get me the Sprite, leaving me just enough time to chat with the folks.

Then, Dorothy dropped bombshell number two. "STUIE, GET DOWN HERE!" Stuart, Dorothy's other younger brother, came racing down the stairs. "Jeremy is sick, and I want you to go to the store to get him some Sprite."

"We have some 7-Up in the fridge. Plus, I'm getting ready for a date."

"Stuart, Jeremy is very sick and he needs Sprite, not 7-Up. Call her and tell her you'll be late. Now go to the store and pick up some Sprite."

Stuart grudgingly reached for the phone and shot me a glance that said I had some explaining to do when Big Sis was not around. I was floored. I didn't understand how such a noble recovery could go unrewarded. I weakly stood up and made my way to the kitchen, feeling quite ill by this point. Ralph was sitting there waiting for me. "Whatever you do, don't tell her you need something else. She'll send me next. If we need to talk, let's talk quietly right now."

Not exactly as planned, but I was out of options and losing credibility fast. "Uh, can I marry Dorothy?"

With a tone that seemed to question why I had gone through such an effort for an old southern formality that hadn't been practiced in the North for at least a hundred years, he replied, "Yes. Did you think we would say no? Now go in the bedroom and ask her mother."

I figured that went well, though it was quite different from the lengthy *mano y mano* discussion I had prepared for. I entered the room where Ellen was sitting, quickly explained what was going on, and sprung the big question on her. The response was memorable.

"Of course you can marry her, Jeremy, but if you ever hurt my Dorothy Ann, I will hunt you down like a dog and shoot you."

Again, not quite what I was expecting, but it sounded fair enough to me, and I figured at this point I should leave well enough alone.

Not to be outdone by the rest of my soon-to-be in-laws, Michael returned from the video store, smiled at his sister, shot me a sneer, and then proudly proclaimed, "They were sold out of *Gladiator*, so I got *Pretty Woman* instead. Dorothy, I know how much you enjoy that movie."

How had it come to this? I had envisioned congratulatory cigars on the back porch. Instead, I got threatened with firearms. I had planned on watching Russell Crowe kick some serious ass. Now, I was facing the fiftieth forced viewing of Julia Roberts meeting some good-looking billionaire and living happily ever after. Surely things could only go up from here.

And they did. As a Christmas/Hanukah present, Ralph and Ellen reserved us a hotel room overlooking Central Park. I planned to take advantage of this golden opportunity and ask Dorothy to marry me. It was a beautiful room, and the sun was setting over the park about the time we checked in. I had originally planned to ask her after dinner but found that the view was too pretty, and I too nervous, to wait. I pulled two chairs in front of the window and ordered wine and cheese from room service (on Ralph's and Ellen's tab, of course). As we sipped our wine and nibbled on the cheese, I asked Dorothy what she was thinking about. I have no idea how she replied because I couldn't hear her over my own pounding heart-beat. When she finished, she asked me what I was thinking about…right on cue.

"I am thinking about our future together," I said. As I produced a ring-sized box, I don't know who was more nervous. As her trembling fingers opened the box to reveal her engagement ring, I got down on bended knee and asked her to marry me.

After a few private moments, we called her family to share the joyous news. When I got on the phone with her father, he asked, "Well, it's kind of early in the evening. Were you smooth?"

Was I smooth? Hell, my nerves were completely shattered. I couldn't shake visions of my soon-to-be mother-in-law wielding a shotgun in my direction, or my soon-to-be wife ordering me around like one of her brothers. All things considered, I thought I was doing remarkably well. "Yeah, I was smooth."

A year and a half later, as our wedding day neared, we decided that we would take our long-anticipated journey as a honeymoon to beat all honeymoons. Without consulting a single travel agent, we threw together a rough itinerary that would take us through Costa Rica, Peru, Chile, Brazil, Argentina, New Zealand, Australia, Singapore, Thailand, Japan, Italy, Germany, and Spain. With little more than two big backpacks, a couple of pairs of hiking boots, and a determination to have a good time, we said farewell to our friends, family, and hard-fought careers and embarked on the adventure of a lifetime.

I am sure many of you have grown tired of receiving the emails and postcards from your buddies telling you what a great time they had on vacation while you were stuck at home. Wouldn't you prefer to read about their pain and suffering caused by sunburns, traveler's diarrhea, and mosquito bites? Wouldn't it be nice to laugh at the truth? Here is your chance.

La Raya

✦

September 5, 2002
Dominical, Costa Rica

Our adventure began in Dominical, a small surfing village on the southern Pacific coast of Costa Rica. After a typical morning of fighting to paddle out against the waves only to be pounded into the ocean floor when attempting to ride them in, I finally decided to take a break. On my way back to shore, I stepped on some sort of pissed-off marine wildlife who thanked me by delivering a punishing blow to my left foot. I stumbled to the beach, fighting to retain consciousness, and crashed on the sand to assess the damage. At that point, it was hard to tell what had happened. There was too much blood and grit to find the actual wound. As I crawled back towards town, I was approached by a lifeguard who determined the culprit was *"una raya"*—a stingray. He helped me back up to my beach bungalow and whipped together a concoction of hot water and local plant leaves. He soaked my foot in the herb juice, and I helped myself to about ten aspirin as Dorothy watched the whole thing with one of those looks that said, "I told your ass you should have been taking Spanish classes, not surfing lessons."

As things calmed down a bit, I asked the lifeguard, who had surfed every day for seven years, and my instructor, who had surfed every day for eight years, if they had ever stumbled across one of these bad boys. They both assured me they hadn't, and that I was extremely "lucky" to have such an experience in only five days.

Now, for those of you who don't have fifteen years to randomly roam the beach all day in the hope of experiencing the wrath of a stingray for yourself, never fear. I will describe a few simple, easy-to-follow steps to replicate the experience in the comfort of your own abode.

1. Attach a 1/8-inch drill bit to a Black and Decker power drill. Place the bit against the back of your heel at a 45-degree angle and, applying firm pressure, start drilling to create a ¾-inch puncture in your foot.

2. Now, a bit of a marine biology lesson here. Stingrays have two barbs on the tail. The first creates the puncture as replicated in step 1, but the second slices the victim. To simulate the effects of the second barb, take a box cutter and, starting at the original puncture wound, create a ¼-inch-deep slash down to about the middle of the sole of your foot.

3. Now that you have properly replicated the initial attack, it is important to experience the walk back into the beach. Start by taking a bucket and filling it up halfway with sand. Then, fill it to the brim with water, adding about two cups of salt for good measure. Place the wounded foot into the bucket and walk in place for two minutes as a friend smacks you in the back with a couch cushion to simulate the waves crashing into you.

4. Ah, but the fun continues, because stingrays are venomous creatures, and you surely don't want to shortchange yourself the fun to be had when the venom spreads throughout your body. The best simulation strategy here is to soak the leg of the wounded foot in ice water for about five minutes. Then, pull it out of the water and beat it all over with a meat tenderizer until you have achieved a proper, holistic throbbing sensation. Repeat for about two hours. Be sure to crank the heater up to about 100 degrees and turn on a Spanish radio station to help simulate the confusion that sets in.

The next day I traded in my surfboard for a fishing pole. I was determined to have my vengeance—for dinner.

To Grandmother's House We Go

◆

September 21, 2002
Monteverde, Costa Rica

Well, I never caught that stingray, and before long it was time to pack up our bags and head inland to Monteverde, Costa Rica. I started to get a little worried that my run-in with our ferocious, fishy friend might prove to be the highlight of my travel humor, leaving me with very little material for the rest of the trip. But never fear, for I would soon get myself into another situation worthy of sharing with the audience at home.

I'll start with a bit of background: Dorothy studied Spanish for about five years in high school and college. Since the beginning of the trip, she has attended intensive private lessons for about four hours a day. She has taken her learning very seriously, spending two to three hours a night studying and doing her home-work. By the time we arrived in Monteverde, Dorothy's Spanish was fluent enough to strike up a conversation with the locals about almost anything.

I studied Spanish for two years in high school and specifically chose an undergraduate degree in business to avoid having to take it in college. In Dominical, I sat through one week of group lessons with a surfer who I believe was stoned most the time. I copied the assignments from some other girl in my class and took long naps while pretending to study as Dorothy did her homework. Needless to say, my Spanish never quite evolved past the spring-break-college-student-in-Cancun proficiency. This pretty much limited my conversations with the locals to a big smile and replies of *pura vida*, which directly translates to 'pure life' and can be used in Costa Rica as an upbeat greeting, farewell, adjective, or exclamation.

That pretty much brings us up to my second morning of Spanish classes in Monteverde where I was staring blankly at my *professora* as she rambled something in *Espanol* that lost me in the first five seconds. Suddenly she stopped, and with a look that could be interpreted as either determination or disgust, said to me, "Jeremy, if you are going to improve in Spanish, you have to practice speaking. Why don't you start with your host family?"

Great, I thought. Finally something in English. This sounded like good advice. So far, my involvement with the family had been limited to watching soccer with the dad and winning the son's lunch money in arm-wrestling competitions[1], neither of which required much verbal interaction. So it was decided—I would make an earnest attempt to strike up conversation with the family.

After dinner that evening, Junior, the father, stepped out on the porch for an after-dinner smoke. I decided this was my chance to practice speaking without having Dorothy, our host mother, Maria, and all the little children around to laugh at my eager but meager attempts to throw together a conversation using my twenty-word vocabulary.

I came out swinging, "Hola, Junior. Que pasa?" (*Hello, Junior. What's up?*)

"Nada. Y usted?" (*Nothing. And you?*) He was testing the waters.

"Nada." Hmmm…was about fresh out of things to say…had to stay with him. "Sus padres viven cerca de aqui?" (*Do your parents live close to here?*) Not exactly the same as discussing sports, but it would do.

"Sí, mi madre vive muy cerca de aqui. Manana, usted quiere ir a su casa?" (*Yes, my mother lives very close to here. Tomorrow, do you want to go to her house?*)

Wow, I was unstoppable. My Spanish was gold. He had taken me in as one of his own. "Sí, me gusta mucho, pero yo tengo escuela a las ocho de la manana." (*Yes, I would love to, but I have school at 8:00 in the morning.*)

---

1.   He is five

Off came the gloves and he hit me with a powerful right hook—two minutes of blindingly fast Spanish. I understood nothing, but I assumed by his smile and good humor that he had said something to the effect of, *That's fine. We will go in the afternoon.* I fell back into the safety zone…big smile. "Pura vida."

He then stood up and went inside. About the time I had convinced myself that I had offended his mother and that he had gone to get his gun, he returned, still wearing a smile, but also wearing a rain jacket. OK, I might be a little slow, but I was starting to get the picture, or so I thought. He had asked if I wanted to go to his mother's house *right now.* Well, I supposed now was as good a time as any, so I went inside, grabbed my rain jacket, and met him back on the front porch.

I headed down the steps of the porch and into the street, only to look up and find no Junior in sight. For the second time in five minutes, I stood there wondering what I was missing. Then, the situation became crystal clear. Out rolled Junior on the 1982 Yamaha 200DT motorcycle, with all-terrain tires and off-road suspension.

Monteverde is located in a very tropical zone that receives about two hours of heavy rain every day. It sits at 5000 feet above sea level and is literally in the clouds. Most evenings, cloud cover is so dense that visibility is reduced to about ten feet. This night was no exception. Most roads outside the town center are a slushy mixture of mud and gravel, with plenty of water-filled potholes and obtrusive large rocks. Since this is a very mountainous region, most roads are quite steep. The closest thing to a streetlight is the soft warm glow of the Imperial Cerveza sign coming from Amigos Bar, which is about a mile away. Monteverde is one of the most beautiful places on earth, but the last place I would want to ride a motorbike at night.

Well, what to do? Motorcycles are the normal means of transportation for everyone who lives around here, so Junior would definitely not understand my turning down his invitation at this point. Plus, he said her house was very close. So I jumped on, and off we went.

Now, I have done my fair share of dangerous activities (skydiving, bungee jumping, eating sushi in Texas), but I have never known fear like on the back of that bike. After a death-defying one-minute ride, he pulled into the *supermercado.* We both got off the bike, and he headed into the store while I stood there with my heart pounding. Then, for the first time in my life I truly appreciated that any bad situation could always become worse—it started pouring.

It was not fifteen seconds later that Junior emerged from the store, and I was reminded again of this new lesson in life. He was holding a bag of pastries, a common token gift when visiting someone's house in Costa Rica, and he passed them to me to hold during the ride to his mother's.

So, off we went again, in the dark of the night, at the mercy of the pouring rain, me hanging on with one hand for ten minutes of sliding through mud, bouncing over rocks, and flying down steep descents. I was praying in both Spanish and English.

Junior seemed none too concerned, and even kept some friendly dialogue flowing. "Hay mucha neblina, sí?" (*There is a lot of fog, isn't there?*)

Yeah, there is so much fog that I can't see the back of your head, which doesn't do a lot for my confidence in your ability to see those big rocks in the road. "Sí, hay mucha neblina."

He knows he's got me. "Hay mucha lluvia, sí?" (*There is a lot of rain, isn't there?*)

Yeah, there is so much rain that I can't tell if I have pissed myself or if I am just soaked through. "Sí, hay mucha lluvia."

He goes for the knockout punch. "Espero que nosotros no chocamos! (*I hope we don't crash!*)

What the hell did that guy just say? Oh, forget trying to speak Spanish, I am just going to worry about holding on. With no smile I replied, "Pura vida."

His mother turned out to be a gracious host, and on the ride back I was considerably less nervous than on the ride out…until we arrived home and I saw Dorothy, whose expression was saying (in English), "Don't you ever attempt to utter one word of Spanish again when I am not with you. Now get inside and do your homework."

I looked at her, big smile. "Pura vida."

Troubled Waters

✦

September 29, 2002
Pacuare River, Costa Rica

After completing our Spanish lessons in Monteverde, Dorothy and I headed to the northern Pacific coast for a final week of study and relaxation on the beach. Time passed quietly, and we soon found ourselves en route to San Jose to check out the nation's capital for a couple of days before flying to Peru. Note to all readers thinking of traveling to Costa Rica: forty-eight hours in San Jose is about forty-six hours too many. There is, however, a great place in town to eat lunch. Namely, the backseat of a "Tourismo" van as the chauffer drives as fast as possible between the airport and the out-of-town beach destination of your choice.

Now, I must admit, I didn't get out and have a stroll around the city, so I am probably not giving it a fair chance. However, I don't think I am completely off the mark. First, I never met anyone from Costa Rica who had a good thing to say about San Jose. When it was mentioned in conversation, their bodies would stiffen, and they would become very intense and serious, launching into a thirty-minute tirade about how my bags and wallet would surely be stolen. OK, I will allow that most people who live in smaller communities have negative things to say about large cities, but consider this. Our hotel in San Jose was in the middle of a shopping center, surrounded by a twelve-foot barbed-wire fence. Patrolling the parking lot, which might have held 500 cars, were no less than twenty security guards armed with shotguns and pistols. After checking in, we went to the receptionist and asked what there was to do around town. He proceeded to tell us about all the different shops and restaurants in the local shopping center. When I asked what there was in the city outside of this specific shopping center, his response was memorable: "Señor, you do not want to go outside the perimeter fencing. We cannot guarantee your safety there."

I am sure San Jose is lovely, but Costa Rica has so much to offer in terms of natural beauty. I definitely thought I could do better than spending a day scampering around downtown with my wallet duct-taped to my ass while my receptionist phoned the American embassy informing them that two hotel guests had ventured beyond the safety of their little caged sanctuary to the certain death that awaited them outside the fencing. So we did as all brave modern-day adventure travelers do; we consulted the Internet.

National Geographic recently ranked Costa Rica's lower Pacuare River as one of the top five white-water rafting trips in the world. This was based on a host of factors, including the difficulty and excitement of the rapids, consistency of water levels, natural beauty, climate, friendliness of the locals (are there little kids sitting on rocks playing "who can hit the tourist with a poison dart?"), and the predatory tendencies of the river wildlife.

Dorothy and I had never been white-water rafting, and conveniently, several tour operators were available to arrange a river trip, which included pick-up and drop-off at our hotel in San Jose. So I decided to give them a call and see what they had to offer.

I lead with something I had been working on in Spanish class the previous week: "Hola, quiero comprender a cerca de sus viajes en el Rio Pacuare?" (I never really knew exactly what this meant.)

"I am sorry, sir. What did you say?" the agent responded.

"You speak English! Outstanding! I want to know about your rafting trips on the Pacuare River."

"We have a full-day trip which runs the lower Pacuare River over some class-3 and class-4 rapids. Have you ever been rafting before, sir?"

"No, but I spent a lot of time last summer floating in my swimming pool in an inflatable lounger." I paused, waiting for laughter.

No laughter. "I see. Well, rapids are rated between one and five, with five being the most difficult. The trip we offer is possible for people with no previous experience, but it is very challenging."

I figured it couldn't be more turbulent than the streets of downtown San Jose (which didn't even receive an honorable mention in the *National Geographic* rafting article), so I signed us up for the trip the following day. Dorothy and I spent the evening marveling at the miracles of modern technology provided by our hotel: remote-controlled television, toilets in which you could flush toilet paper[1], and, perhaps the holiest of holies, air conditioning.

We awoke in the morning well-rested and ready to tackle the challenge of the day. After quickly getting ready, we waited outside for our bus to pick us up, well within the safety afforded by the hotel's barbed-wire fences and small army. The bus was only an hour late, which was well within the generally accepted three hour window that is considered "on time" in Costa Rica.

After a beautiful three-hour ride through vibrant-emerald forests, we arrived at the river, where we were introduced to our raft guide. This guy was straight out of a Nike commercial. I wouldn't have been at all surprised if he'd had a swoosh tattooed on his back. He was deeply tanned with bleached highlights in his dark, spiky hair. He was on Costa Rica's national rafting team and looked like he ran a marathon every morning to warm up before his six or seven hours of paddling. He was hype, cool, hard, extreme, athletic, and crazy. And he knew it.

It became very clear in the fifteen-minute introduction that while on his raft, rafting would not be a pleasant recreational pastime; this was going to be extreme sporting. He would not accept lazy tourists who just wanted to float down the river. This day, and *every* day aboard his raft, was for athletic thrill seekers who could count on spending the rest of the afternoon constantly paddling through a variety of tough, technically-complex maneuvers as directed by his barks from the rear of the boat.

Once we completed the briefing session, we put on our life jackets and helmets and shoved off accompanied by other, perhaps less militant rafts and their squads. Joining our crew was a couple from Holland and a lady from France. The Dutch guy and I were positioned in the front of the raft and were instructed to set a "powerful" pace. Now, for those who haven't met many people from the Netherlands, they are generally very tall. The average man is about six-foot four (well, almost), and this guy was no exception. Additionally, it looked like he spent his weekends and evenings bench-pressing cars and arm wrestling bears. He

---

1.   I flushed a whole roll just for fun.

was a monster. His version of a powerful pace and mine differed slightly. Additionally, he had two people on his side of the boat helping him (his girlfriend and the French lady), whereas I only had one (Dorothy).

It wasn't five minutes into the trip that the white-water-commando started in on me: "Stronger pace on the left front, Jeremy." Two minutes later: "Stronger pace on the left." One minute later: "We need more power on the left."

I started off a little skeptical of this clown. Those feelings were quickly escalating to a vocal hostility. Not to mention that I was completely not up for five more hours of paddling for my life while being orally horse-whipped to go faster.

"We need to speed it up on the left."

I lost it. "Look, bud, I am paddling as fast as I can. Unless you got a little outboard motor in your bag of tricks back there, you are not going to get any more power on the left. I also have a couple of other observations. If we don't paddle at all, the river does seem to be taking us in the right direction. And finally, instead of more power on the left, less power on the right would have the same effect. If I hear one more thing out of you about more power on the left, I am going to wrap this paddle around your head."

OK, so I didn't say this, mainly because psycho-boy looked like he would have come out his seat and whipped my ass. Instead, I opted for the equally effective, less confrontational approach. I chose to ignore him.

This seemed to work pretty well until we approached the first rapid, at which point he was making so much noise that I thought our raft had come under fire by enemy aircraft. I decided it was time to tune back in.

"Back left, back left, BACK LEFT!"

I was now rowing backward as hard as I could, but it proved to be too little, too late. A six-foot wall of water knocked us completely sideways. Then everything seemed to happen in slow motion. The hulk from Holland was thrown from his seat and landed right on top of me. Dorothy had gone overboard. The raft was flipping over. For the slightest instant before I submerged, I made eye contact with the guide. To say he looked upset might be one of the greatest understatements of all time. I thought there was a very real possibility he would swim over and break my neck while we were underwater.

As we resurfaced, one of the rescue kayaks had already made its way over to me. "Get Dorothy first," I screamed in an attempt to be manly.

"Stand up!" He shouted back. I was in about three feet of water.

Meanwhile, the other rafts rescued Dorothy and the rest of our crew. When we reconvened on the bank, I prepared myself for the berating I was due from the guide. Instead, he came over, and with the smile of a lunatic, said, "Yeah guys! I love it when that happens! You guys rock!" Like I said, clearly insane.

After the flip, the French lady, who I don't think quite realized what she had signed up for, pretty much lay down in the back of the boat, not even holding a paddle, but rather gripping the safety ropes for dear life. With the balance of paddlers equaled at two a side, Dorothy and I were able to hold our own and the guide let up on me.

After several more hours successfully navigating rapids, we returned to San Jose to marvel at another feature of the modern hotel: a comfortable bed and a good night's sleep.

Where Is the Oxygen?

✦

October 14, 2002
Cuzco, Peru

Cuzco, Peru is nestled in the Andes at 11,444 feet above sea level.[1] To provide perspective, Denver, Colorado, rests at a mere 5,500 feet. At altitudes over 10,000 feet, the air is so thin that one must start to worry about the Big A. No not alcoholism, acne, or anxiety attacks, but altitude sickness. For those who are not familiar with altitude sickness, I have taken the liberty to track down the following definition from the New England Journal of Medicine (the Special Wise-Ass Edition):

---

1.   Give or take a foot

Altitude sickness is an illness that may occur when a person ascends to an altitude in excess of 10,000 feet for an extended period of time and is caused by a lack of oxygen reaching the brain. This malady strongly resembles the worst hangover imaginable, lasting for about three days, leaving the victim whimpering like a baby and crying out for his or her mother. Symptoms include:

- A headache similar to what one would expect from trying to catch a Nolan Ryan fastball with one's forehead

- Nausea that one would associate with eating a half pound of rotten raw hamburger meat, then chugging a gallon of milk left festering in the sun, and topping it off with a Tabasco-flavored after-dinner mint and a big wad of teriyaki-flavored chewing tobacco

- Mental confusion and disorientation similar to the post trauma of a stingray attack.

By now you've probably guessed it: I spent the first couple of days in Cuzco in pretty bad shape. It all started at five in the morning the day after we arrived. After a restless first night spent trying to adjust to the altitude, I stumbled into the bathroom and sat on the commode. I felt horrible. Suddenly, a wave of pain pulsed through my head. I blacked out, falling forward off the toilet and face-planting on the bathroom tile. Dorothy heard me hit the deck and rushed into the bathroom to check on me. In a display of grand heroics, she burst through the bathroom door, slamming it into the side of my face as I lay there. This proved a very effective technique for helping me regain consciousness.

When I came around, I couldn't remember anything. I assessed the situation. I was curled up in the fetal position on the bathroom floor of some dodgy hotel with my face battered and my boxers down around my ankles. Dorothy was standing over me looking down. "Oh, jeez. Sorry about your face. Are you OK…did you wipe?"

What in the hell is going on? What did Dorothy do to my face? What is all this about wiping? Why am I half-nude and bleeding? Am I the victim of some bizarre case of perverted spousal abuse? Somebody help me! She's turned on me. I feel so lightheaded. Have I been drugged? Perhaps she plans to sell my organs. I knew I had to be careful in South America, but I thought I could trust Dorothy. Call the embassy! Somebody help!

Finally, it all came back to me. After getting me cleaned up, our first course of action was to seek the treatment recommended by the locals, *maté de coca*. *Maté* has been used as a tonic for thousands of years by South Americans and sharing it with foreigners was traditionally seen as an honored social custom. This beverage is prepared by pouring hot water on the actual coca leaves themselves, giving the whole experience a bit of an "earthy bohemian flare," as one fellow backpacker described it. So Dorothy and I headed to a café to give it a try. Earthy, yes. Bohemian, possibly. Anything close to a remedy for my ailments? Not by a long shot. Being the capital-minded cynic that I am, I have my own little theory about the recent local commercialization of *maté de coca*, and it goes something like this:

One day some smart locals realized they could take their yard clippings, pour hot water over them, and then serve it to idiot backpackers who would happily pay $1 for this funky brew. Surprised by the overwhelming success, these entrepreneurs decided to tell gullible travelers that the yard-clipping infusion was actually the revered *maté de coca*, which was known to help ease the ailments of altitude sickness. Demand took off like wildfire, and our self-starters began raking and bagging all the dead leaves they could find and selling them to all the other cafés in town.

As I staggered out of the café, feeling worse than I had earlier[2], one of the local children rushed up to Dorothy and me and aggressively attempted to sell us post cards, sweaters, jewelry and a whole cart full of other items I had no use for. I bared my teeth and growled at him, struggling to keep my balance while Dorothy politely told him (in perfect Spanish) that all of his items were very beautiful, but that we did not want to buy anything because I was not feeling well.

Then it hit me. Even with blurred eyesight, I could make out dozens, if not hundreds, of other travelers who appeared to be in just as bad of shape as I was. They all had young street vendors hounding them to buy souvenirs. But what did these people really want? What one thing would I, and all my fellow afflicted travelers, happily trade all our worldly possessions for? The answer, my friends: one deep, slow, deliberate pull from a canister of pure oxygen—the only true proven relief for altitude sickness.

What this town needed was a huge oxygen factory. I could crank out thousand of canisters of oxygen a day, and then use these young street vendors to move the product. They had all the sales skills down pat, so it would take me no time to train them:

"OK, kid, you set the price at 250 bucks a canister. Now, nobody is going to pay that price. So, what you do is you give them a taste for free. 'Here, mister, just try it. The first breath is on me.' You watch as his eyes glaze over and the headache seems to melt right out of him. Then you watch as his newly-formed smile starts to fade into a frown and then a panic. As he cries for some more, you tell him that you only have one canister left, so it is going to cost him 350 green-

---

2.   Probably due to a bit of poison ivy in my yard-clipping mock *maté*

backs...but no problem, you take credit! Then you slide his Visa through the little machine you wear around your waist and complete the transaction. Your inventory levels will automatically be updated in our central systems and we will come by in a van to supply you with more product when you are getting low."

Before anyone knew what had happened, I would be running the biggest oxygen cartel in South America, spending my afternoons having drinks with the *maté de coca* yard-clipping czar and toasting our newly-found empires.

The Second Day of the Inca Trail

✦

October 24, 2002
Machu Picchu, Peru

The Inca Trail is a twenty-seven-mile hike, which is usually conquered in a four-day/three-night trek. Common practice is to sign up with a local tour group, who will provide a guide, cook, and group of porters who will jointly carry and prepare all the tents and food at each campsite. This leaves you to carry your clothes, sleeping bag and mat, medical kit, daily snacks, water, and personal items (suntan lotion, camera, inferred night-vision goggles, navy seal all-purpose combat knife, kinetically-charged palm-size GPS system, etc). Dorothy and I (more Dorothy) opted to take one small pack to carry the water, snacks, and camera, which she carried, and then one humongous 6000-cubic-inch-monster for everything else, which yours truly ended up with. On the scales, my pack weighed 40 lbs—on the trail it felt more like 45 lbs—but given the uncertainty, we'll call it an even 50, just to be on the safe side.

So off we went on the first day, trekking at a steady pace, talking with our fellow hikers and trying to get a better feel for the challenge ahead. Within the first thirty minutes, I met an older lady who was hiking the trail with another tour group, and we started chatting about the adventure on which we had just embarked. When she told me she was sixty-two, my confidence soared. If she could make it, then it shouldn't be any problem for this strong, strapping Texas man in his mid-twenties. She then continued to tell me how she had trained by hiking fifty miles a week for the last four months. I almost tripped. My regimen had been more along the lines of drinking beer on the beach in Costa Rica. When she asked how I had trained, I told her I had hiked 100 miles a week for the past year carrying a 75-lb pack, then walked on in front of her before the fear in my eyes gave me away.

Two things really caught my attention on day one: the stunning natural beauty of the trail and the athletic ability of the porters. After we had finished our lunches and headed back onto the trail, these guys would stay behind to clean up the dishes, strip down the tents and repack the gear, a feat which I would guess took thirty or forty-five minutes. They would then literally run the trail, each packing 75+ lbs, pass us along the way, and arrive at the next campsite early enough to have set up the tents and prepared a pre-dinner snack by the time we arrived…quite a humbling experience.

That evening when we arrived at the campsite, my legs were shot, my shoulders were throbbing, and my pack felt like it weighed more than I did. After dinner it was straight to bed for a much-needed rest. We awoke the next day to face the most difficult leg of the trail—a three-mile hike climbing 3600 feet to a peak at 15,500 feet called Dead Woman's Pass. (I was too scared to ask how it got its name.) And all of this was to be done in the morning, before lunch.

I was near tears at the thought of having to strap back on the monster, when Dorothy spoke words of pure poetry. "Jeremy, my back is kind of hurting. I think I am going to hire a porter to carry my pack. Perhaps we should have the porter carry your big bag, and you can carry this smaller one."

What a blessing! I could retain my strong, strapping-Texas-man image and not have to tote the colossus. "Well, I could probably carry them both, honey (like hell)…but then I couldn't take many pictures. Of course we will hire you a porter." Sweet! I quickly asked the guide how much it would be to have a porter tote the monster—$8. Sucker. I would have paid $100. Heck, at $8 for the bag, I considered asking him how much it would cost to have the porters carry me. I mean, that would be the way to travel in style. I could picture it clearly. "Faster down there…OK, now stop at this scenic overlook so I can take some pictures. Could you hand my water up to me…I get really hot in this sun. Thanks."

So off we went. Without a small house on my back, I was able to really focus on getting some great pictures. I was going to great lengths to get the perfect action shots—charging ahead of the group, climbing trees, scaling the side of the mountain, whatever it took to get the perfect angle. After about an hour of convincing myself that I would return to the work force as a photographer for *National Geographic*, Dorothy politely told me that if I took one more picture of her while she was sweaty and gross, she would throw me off the side of the mountain. So away went the cameras for a while.

At the final group resting point before the pass, I rekindled my aspirations of photographic glory and told Dorothy to continue ahead while I changed the film and switched lenses. "I will be right behind you and will catch up in about ten minutes." Now, the entire morning of the second day was a very challenging hike, but unbeknownst to me, the final hour from the resting point to the pass would be a complete killer.

As I charged off at a brisk pace to catch up with Dorothy, I quickly felt the effects of the altitude coupled with the steep incline of the trail. Ten minutes passed and I thought, "OK, so it might take twenty to catch her." Twenty soon became thirty, thirty forty, and finally I realized that I would not be catching up with her and the group before the pass. I was panting like a sled dog and needed a break.

As I resumed the climb after my break, my goal was no longer to catch Dorothy, but to just to make it to the top. After 100 steps I needed another break. My legs started to tremble and my breathing was very rapid. "OK, kid, dig deep, let's do fifty steps, then break, fifty then break, all the way to the top." This worked for about ten minutes, and then the old legs quit working. "Hmmm…OK, kid, give me forty steps then you get a break and some water." I got another five minutes out of this approach…but no more. "All right, big man, thirty steps and then a break with water and some chocolate." A couple more minutes of progress, but the body couldn't take any more. The air was just too thin for someone who honed his fitness practicing the extreme sport of sunbathing. I could see the top now. I was only maybe 200 steps from the peak, but the legs just wouldn't cooperate. "Come on, fat boy; get your butt up this mountain!" Nothing going. I saw Dorothy at the peak. She waved at me. I was sad, for I knew I might never see her again as the final challenge was proving insurmountable.

I sat there contemplating how much an emergency airlift off that mountain was going to cost me. Then, an amazing thing happened. A small man, weighing no more than a buck twenty, who I recognized as one of our porters, came running by me toting my monster pack, all the tents strapped to the sides, and a huge fuel tank strapped to the back. He bounded up the final 200 feet to the pass and continued down the trail without even taking a break at the top.

Stunned, I got up and starting walking, thinking to myself, "That might well be the best $8 I ever spent." Before I knew it, I was at the top at the pass making up some excuse about how I had stopped to take some pictures.

Brimming with the confidence from the ascent, Dorothy and I carried our original packs for the remainder of the trip and were delighted with the rewarding views of Machu Picchu a few days later.

Oh yeah, and I beat the old grandma by thirty minutes! Maybe instead of a *National Geographic* photographer, I should work on the Inka Trail as a porter. Hmmm…well, maybe not.

Ode to Big Mac

✦

October 28, 2002
Arica, Chile

I recently had an experience so moving that it drove me to poetry.

(To the melody of "'Twas the Night before Christmas")

> We gathered our bags
> As we pulled into the station.
> "Are we finally in Chile,
> That long skinny nation?"
>
> "That's correct," Dorothy answered.
> "Now go ask that man
> How much to take us
> To town in his van."
>
> We agreed on a price
> And away we all went,
> At which point occurred
> A most incredible event.
>
> For far on the hill
> I saw a deep amber glow,
> And I exclaimed with great joy,
> "It's the Golden Arches, yo!"

After no American food
For sixty-one days,
I pushed through the doors
In a delirious craze.

I rushed to the counter,
As there wasn't a line,
"Two Big Mac meals please,
And super-size mine!"

Ode to joy and beauty
And everything nice.
Ode to burgers and fries
And no black beans and rice.

Two all-beef patties,
Special sauce, lettuce, cheese,
All consumed in three bites,
"Another Big Mac please."

We laughed and we giggled
As we enjoyed our feast.
And it felt good to be home,
For one meal at least.

For those traveling abroad
When homesickness gets dire,
The sun never sets
On the McDonald's empire.

Back in the Saddle

✦

November 2, 2002
Atacama Desert, Chile

The Atacama Desert in Northern Chile is one of the most inhospitable terrains imaginable. First, it is dry. Real dry. The kind of dry that causes your lips to crack, skin to turn scaly, and tongue to feel like leather. During the day, it is hot. Scorching hot. I am not talking about the ninety-five-degree heat that would send your average person into severe heat stroke. Having grown up in Houston, I laugh at such heat. No, when I speak of scorching, I am talking about well over 110 degrees in the shade. The sort of heat where sunburn is not as much of a concern as spontaneous combustion. Then comes the night, when the temperature plummets to well below freezing—a bone-chilling cold that penetrates the thick adobe walls to punish those ill-prepared travelers who only thought to bring lightweight sleeping sheets. Ahem!

Given the environment, there is not much wildlife in these parts. In fact, the only animals I encountered were a perplexing breed of nomadic mammals known as backpackers. These strange creatures are usually from Europe, North America, Australia, New Zealand, Israel, and Japan. While in Chile, they travel independently, sometimes in pairs, or often in large, annoying groups on a tour bus. They walk on two legs, struggling to support the weight of a huge rucksack, which is always in tote. In one hand, they carry a liter-sized bottle of water, in the other, a heavily-used copy of the *Lonely Planet*. They communicate in English and broken Spanish, mainly discussing such things as hostels, tour companies, Internet cafés, bus schedules, bars, and Thailand (where they all seemed to visit at some point in their journey). They eat trail mix during the day while pretending to be adventurers and switch to sandwiches at night in an attempt to be budget conscious. And they all congregate in a small town in the middle of the desert named San Pedro de Atacama to seek their thrills, tell their tales, and see the sights.

So, there we were in San Pedro trying to select from the dizzying number of adventure excursions offered by a host of different companies. As confusion mounted and the heat grew intolerable, I went back to the basics. "Hello, do you speak English?" The first "yes" I got was the winner.

We sat in the office as the agent explained the adventures, which covered the entire spectrum—from mountain biking to sand-dune surfing. Then, one really caught my attention. Horseback riding. Being a Texan, I have always seen myself as a bit of a cowboy, mainly attributable to my five or six times on a horse as a young kid. I pressed for details.

Seeing the opportunity to close the deal, the agent laid out the trip options. "We have several short one- or two-hour trips for inexperienced riders, but if you are comfortable on a horse, then we offer a really amazing five hour trip. It starts with a trot through a dry creek bed, then continues up to a whispering dark, narrow tunnel that burrows through the mountain, then it's down a sand dune and through Death Valley, and you finish back at the stables right across from the saloon."

I was sold. Dry creek beds, tunnels through mountains, sand dunes, Death Valley—hell, yeah, this was the adventure for me. Dorothy started to protest, "I have never been on a horse before. Five hours is a long time. Is it safe? It sounds kind of dangerous. Jer, maybe we should go on one of the shorter trips."

"Honey, the shorter trips are for sissies. I mean we might as well ride on the merry-go-round. The five-hour trip will be fine. All you have to do is sit there. The horse does all the work. Trust me. Two for the Death Valley trip please."

Dorothy continued to question the decision but knew her concerns were falling on deaf ears, as the lady was already swiping my card and calculating her commission. I was all smiles.

The next morning we showed up at the stables and met our guide. Dorothy immediately confessed, "Look, I have never been on a horse before. The agent said this trip is only for experienced riders. I don't have any experience. Do you think we should go on an easier trip?"

I was panic-stricken. In an instant, I saw my chances of thundering through Death Valley on a stallion replaced by riding in circles on a pony. I started to speak but was cut off by the guide. "No problem. We have a very calm, gentle horse who is very good with beginners. Her name is Bonita. I am sure you will have no problems with her." With these words of reassurance, the man disappeared into the stable. He returned with a truly magnificent show champion of a horse. Her gait was noble, her coat shone, and her mane blew freely in the wind. She looked like a Budweiser Clydesdale as she stood before us, eager to greet her new rider. Dorothy was immediately more at ease as the guide helped her into her saddle.

I was ready to meet my horse, so I turned to the guide. "I am from Texas (true). I ride horses almost daily (big exaggeration). Hell, I took first place in a rodeo when I was eight (complete lie). I want a strong, fast horse that will be able to keep up with me (true, though a bit self delusional)."

The guide gave me a quick look over and then a smile. "Very good, sir. I have just the right horse for you. His name is Frank." The man disappeared into the stable and returned with Frank.

Frank looked nothing like the magnificent Bonita. In fact, he didn't look much like a horse at all. He looked more like a mix between a bucktoothed donkey and a cross-eyed llama. He sort of staggered when he walked and appeared to have been on the losing end of a bar fight the night before. It was obvious that he was more than a little upset to be up this early, and I thought I smelled whiskey on his breath.

I appealed to the guide, "Uh, Frank isn't quite the horse I had in mind."

"Don't worry, Frank is our fastest horse. You will love him." And with that, he climbed into his saddle and stared me down until I did the same. The trip started slowly as we made our way through the creek bed. The guide rode in front, Dorothy right behind him on Bonita, and I took it up the rear on Frank, who had stumbled off to the side, seeming as if he might puke or collapse. Not wanting to fall behind the others, I gave Frank a good kick. Nothing. I pulled on his reins, trying to steer him back into line. No response.

"What's this guy's problem," I wondered. I gave him a final hard pull on the reins. He stopped, turned his head, stared at me with a fiery eye, and blew smoke from his nostrils. The message was clear. *You so much as touch me with your boots or lay another hand on those reins, and I will buck you off and stomp on your head.*

I knew then and there that Frank was in the driver's seat. I was merely along for the ride.

However, with this little exchange complete, Frank galloped right up behind Dorothy and Bonita. Well that was more like it. Maybe I had misinterpreted things and Frank was actually ready to behave. Maybe he saw something in my eyes that scared him. Perhaps he saw the hawkish resolve of a big, strong Texan man riding high in his saddle who would give him a good ass-whooping if he didn't fall in line. Sitting tall in my saddle, I smiled with pride, knowing that I had shown him who was boss.

I was about to take the reigns back in my hand when the reality of the situation hit me. While Bonita was a beautiful horse, she had apparently eaten a breakfast that did not agree with her. She had horrible gas.

Every fifteen seconds she released a little toxic burst that left me gagging. Frank would let out a little snort that sounded like a chuckle. The torture of the fumes coupled with the unrelenting sun rapidly became unbearable. I yanked furiously on the reins in a vain attempt to escape to a more oxygen-rich, chemical-free environment. No luck. I finally called to Dorothy in crazed desperation and she steered Bonita to the side, allowing Frank to pass.

The next several hours were thankfully peaceful as Frank stumbled along at whatever pace he pleased, and I enjoyed the breathtaking scenery of the desert. Then we came to the tunnel—the 'whispering dark narrow tunnel,' as the tour agent had described it earlier. It turned out *whispering* actually meant gusting-seventy-mile-per-hour winds. *Dark* was more like pitch black. And *narrow* probably would have been better described prefixed by *very.*

But off we went anyway, and soon Frank returned to his old antics. About fifty feet into the tunnel, he veered about a foot to the left of the line the guide was taking. At this new position, my left leg was scraping the jagged, rocky wall of the tunnel. Now, these horses walked this trail daily, so I have to think old Frank knew the anguish he was causing me. I went through my well-practiced routine of pulling on his reins as I cursed him in English and Spanish, but all to no avail, as I could not even hear myself over the roaring wind.

I emerged from the tunnel with a scraped leg, torn jeans, and a heightened hostility for my tormentor. I longed for an Indiana Jones-style whip so I could extract a bit of revenge. Alas, I had left my whip in my hotel room (next to my night-vision goggles) and was left seething in the blistering sun as we plodded forward towards the sand dunes.

When we got to the top of the dunes, I was shocked. I had envisioned gentle rolling dunes, something like a sandy version of the Texas Hill Country. This was more like a double black-diamond ski slope where to fall would mean thirty seconds of bone-snapping tumbling followed by my slow, lingering death as buzzards hovered to feast on my remains. I wouldn't do this on foot and was horrified of the thought of being at Frank's mercy.

Dorothy and Bonita went first. Bonita was slow and steady, attempting to comfort the unease of her rider. As they disappeared out of sight, Frank didn't budge an inch.

"I am with you, bud. Screw that. Let's just stay right her until we figure out another way down." I had almost forgiven him as I leaned up to give him a pat on the neck. Then to my absolute horror, he reared back on two legs, raced to the edge of the cliff and jumped as if trying to clear a fence. My heart stopped beating, and I probably would have screamed if I could have breathed.

As we raced down the near-vertical slope, immediately passing Dorothy and the guide, I held on for dear life. Frank continued to gain momentum, obviously pleased with my terror. As he charged onward, my camera, which had been safely hanging around my neck, swung violently, busting my lip and somehow cutting my knuckles in the process. When my companions finally joined me at the bottom, the guide gave me a five-minute lecture about how I needed to keep tension on the reins. If I'd had a gun, I would have shot him…and then Frank. But once again, it was packed back in my room, right beside my whip. (Just kidding. It was actually under my pillow, where I always keep it.)

As we continued the trip through Death Valley, it occurred to me how fitting the name was, because I truly felt near death. My lip was swollen, my knuckles were bleeding, my jeans were torn, there was a nasty gash on my leg, my man-package ached from too many hours in the saddle, and I felt faint from the merciless heat of the sun. Yes, Death Valley was the perfect name.

When we finally arrived back at the stables, I stumbled off Frank and waddled across the dirt road into the promised saloon. After the bartender handed me a much needed beer, he asked "What happened to you, buddy? You look like you just lost a fight."

I looked him straight in the eye and responded, "Yeah, but you should see the other guy. He looks like mix between a bucktoothed donkey and a cross-eyed llama, and I think the damage is permanent."

He shot Dorothy a look that said, "Where did you find this guy?"

Kayaking with the Jedi Knight

✦

November 6, 2002
Pucon, Chile

After a couple of weeks of baking in Chile's northern desert region, we decided to head south for a cool reprieve in the Chilean Lake District. We were tired of being on the move and opted to enjoy a relaxed week in a cozy lodge on the outskirts of the quaint resort town of Pucon.

Having checked into our accommodations, we set off to find some lunch, randomly strolling through town until we came to a restaurant which served an inviting selection of European and American cuisines. We sat at a table by the window and placed our orders. Dorothy chose a "delightful culinary selection from the Greek Isles" that included salads, olives, couscous, and grape leaves dressed with extra virgin olive oil and a touch of balsamic vinegar. I chose an equally delightful culinary selection from Texas: a bacon-double-cheeseburger, a side of fries, and an ice-cold Budweiser—enough lard and cholesterol to tide me over until dinner.

As we waited for the food to arrive, Dorothy noticed the owners of the restaurant also ran an adventure tour company. We flipped through the brochure, reading about and discussing various options. When the waiter returned with our meals, he noticed our interest in the activities.

"Our most popular excursion is a two-day kayaking class. If you have never been kayaking before, it is a blast."

It wasn't a hard sell. Dorothy and I had really enjoyed our white-water rafting trip in Costa Rica (despite my little episode with the guide), and we were very eager to give kayaking a try. During our previous rafting trip, there had been two additional guides who followed the group in their own kayaks. They were surfing waves, spinning in circles, and performing all sorts of cool tricks. Given that we already had some rafting experience, I was sure that with two days of training, we would look equally impressive in the water.

We ate our lunch and then headed upstairs to make the reservations. As we completed the paperwork, we met our guide, who had been kayaking competitively for twenty years. He calmly described the two-day training course with a sort of meditative coolness that immediately put us at ease. He spoke perfect English, but there was a certain peculiarity about his sentence structure and cadence that gave me a feeling of *deja vu*. It wasn't the typical case of awkward word selection from someone who had yet to master the English language. Rather, he sounded like a wise sage of generations past. Then it hit me. He sounded like Yoda from *Star Wars*.

"Hmmm, masters of kayaking you will become. Fun, you will have, but practice you must." He went on like this for about ten minutes and concluded by telling us he would swing by our hotel and pick us up at 8:00 the following morning. I thought he would part with "May the Force be with you," but he didn't.

The next morning, we climbed into his truck and headed off for the company's cabin, where we would pick up our gear. While he was driving, he handed us a pair of sports goggles and asked us to turn them over and take a look on the back of the package. Upon doing so, we saw a picture of him kayaking through some huge rapids quickly approaching a thirty-foot waterfall. Jedi Knight, possibly. Bad-ass kayaker, definitely.

Once we arrived at the cabin, our first task was to select and adjust our kayaks. Immediately, one point became very clear. River kayaking is not a big man's sport. These boats were tiny.

Yoda sensed my tension. "I feel much fear in you."

"Not fear," I replied. "I just didn't realize how small these kayaks were. I am not sure I am going to fit into one of them." In fact, I could already hear them down in the local bar. "Did you hear about that American that tried to go kayaking today? He couldn't even get his fat ass into the kayak."

After some uncomfortable scrunching and squeezing, I was finally able to wedge myself into the hull. We loaded the boats onto the truck and then made our way inside the cabin to get our wetsuits, helmets, lifejackets, and spray skirts. It's all as bad as it sounds. After gearing up, I looked like a female construction worker on my way to swimming lessons. I'd have made the perfect addition to the Village People.

With gear in place and all dressed for the occasion, we headed to the lake where we would spend the morning practicing our paddling. As we stood at the edge of the water preparing to get into our kayaks, I was a bit disappointed. This lake was dead still; I was expecting rapids. Sure, I knew I needed to practice, but hell, I had been rafting. I thought we should at least be starting in a slow-moving river.

Yoda read my mind. "Patience you must have. Balance you must learn."

He was right. To flip a kayak, you only need to slightly flex a pinky toe or swish a little saliva into one side of your mouth. I lasted approximately 1.8 seconds and then, "Oh, shi-blup-blup-blup!"

Completely humbled, shocked by the freezing water, and more than a little worried about being trapped in this snug upside-down death trap, I shot out of that boat almost as quickly as I managed to flip. As I resurfaced, Dorothy was having a good laugh and Yoda was staring at me in a pensive, knowing manner.

I pushed the boat back to shore and struggled to empty it. Filled with water, kayaks weigh about seventy pounds. Finally, with a little direction from Yoda, I positioned the nose of the boat on the beach and was able to hoist the rear enough to allow the water to drain.

Next, it was Dorothy's turn to flip, an experience which quickly wiped the smile off her face. As she reemerged, she stared at me as if daring me to smile. I wisely resisted the urge. Then I saw the most incredible feat on the trip to date. Our guide, who was in his kayak, took Dorothy's water-filled kayak and balanced it on the nose of his boat. Then, with the strength of a bull and the grace of a swan, he lifted the upside-down kayak over his head, allowing the water to pour out of the hull. He then placed the kayak back in the water, right side up, and pushed it over to Dorothy. I was astonished. My complete surprise caused me to loose my balance and flip over for a second time. No mere human could dead lift seventy pounds of awkward weight above his head, solely relying on upper body strength, while maintaining perfect balance in a kayak. This guy obviously was a Jedi Knight. When I surfaced, I expected to see him place one finger on his temple, hold the other hand in front of him, and use the Force to raise an X-Wing fighter from the middle of the lake.

Once Dorothy and I were comfortable sitting in our kayaks, we advanced to a paddling lesson. First, Yoda demonstrated the correct paddling technique. He glided effortlessly through the glassy water. I wasn't impressed. The water was perfectly calm, so this couldn't be too difficult. Plus, I had already learned to balance, so paddling should prove easy. Wrong. Paddling a kayak is about as easy as driving a car with bald tires on icy roads in the middle of a blizzard without using your steering wheel or brake. I would start off straight, but upon accelerating, would quickly spin out and tip over.

By noon, we had improved slightly and were ready for lunch. We loaded the kayaks into the truck and headed to the cabin. I was famished. I ate a modest lunch of three sandwiches, two oranges, an apple, a bag of chips, a chocolate bar, and half a muffin. Happy and full, we drove to some local hot springs, where we would learn to barrel roll the kayak in a complete circle. This is the preferred alternative to ejecting when the kayak flips over. The correct technique for this maneuver is easily explained:

1. Once you tip over, tuck your head towards your knees into a "safety position." At the same time, place the paddle along the left side of the kayak as far back as possible.

2. Extend your right arm forward across your body.

3. In an explosive manner, rotate your hips to the left and pull your right hand down, rotating the kayak upwards in a counterclockwise motion.

4. If for any reason this doesn't flip you right side up, reach forward and pull the release strap of your spray skirt to eject from the boat.

Simple. Yoda demonstrated effortlessly. We even watched underwater, using the goggles he endorses. It seemed just as easy as he described. "Why had I been ejecting all this time?" I wondered. This seemed much easier.

After a couple of tries, I determined that little inconveniences such as gravity, disorientation, and lack of oxygen are not a problem for a Jedi Knight. As a result, I have rewritten the steps required for a mere human to perform the barrel roll:

1. Do not be alarmed by the gallon of water that just went up your nose. This will slowly drain out over the next few days.

2. Remember that you are upside down and that left is right, down is up, clockwise is counterclockwise, etc. and vice versa.

3. Place the paddle along the left side of the kayak as far back as possible.

4. No, that is the right. Move the paddle to the other side of the boat.

5. Remain calm about the burning sensation in your chest. This is a common condition caused by a lack of oxygen. You will probably faint soon and the pain will ease.

6. Extend your right arm forward across your body.

7. In an explosive manner, rotate your hips to the left and pull your right hand down, smashing the paddle into your face.

8. Of course, this does not flip you over. That was simply a cruel joke that Jedi Knights play on those who have not mastered the Force. The water filling your lungs is becoming problematic. Quickly move to Step 9.

9. Reach forward and pull the release strap of your spray skirt to eject from the boat.

10. Of course, you will not be able to find the release strap. What did you expect? Think about it. You are upside down and close to drowning. Your coordination is about the same as the time you drank five Hurricanes at Mardi Gras. Move quickly to Step 11.

11. Flail your arms like crazy until Yoda rescues you.

And it only got better. After several attempts, I was really wishing I hadn't eaten such a large lunch. All that underwater flailing nauseated me. Once again, I could hear the locals at the bar: "That American finally got his fat ass wedged into the kayak, and then he hurled in the local hot springs while trying to learn the roll. Ha ha ha."

After several rests to let my stomach settle, I finally got to where I could comfortably perform the role 1 out of every 132 tries. That is to say, I did it once. On that note, I ended the day.

The next day we were set to practice running the rapids in a local river. Instead of kayaks, Dorothy and I were going to ride in duckies. Duckies are similar to a kayak, but inflatable and open-topped, like a raft.

Dorothy and I were accompanied by three guides on the river: Yoda, to stay with Dorothy, and two new guides. One was to stay with me, and the other to rove between us.

It was immediately obvious that these two new guides were also amazing kayakers. My guide introduced himself, "I am Raul, and this is my machine, Piranha." His kayak actually had a piranha logo on the side. I shook his hand and pet his kayak. With muscles rippling and tattoos flaring, he continued, "You just follow my lead, and you will do just fine."

Away we went, Yoda in the pole position, Dorothy in a close second, followed by the two new guides, and me bringing up the rear. During the first thirty minutes, we were on fast-moving water, but little to no rapids. We practiced steering the duckies, reading the current, and braking on eddies. This proved quite easy, as the ducky was about 1,400,750 times more stable than a kayak. Then we got into the rapids. These were class-3+ to class-4 rapids, with waves up to six feet tall. The main strategy was to hit the wave straight on and lean into it. If done correctly, the ducky went right over the wave. Done incorrectly and it was time for a swim.

Soon, I found myself struggling to keep the ducky straight. The waves were coming at me from all directions. I looked in front of me and saw Dorothy was struggling as well. I looked in front of her and caught a glimpse of Yoda, who was riding the rapids backwards so he could fully focus on Dorothy. The guy didn't even use his paddle. Incredible.

Dorothy and I battled the rapids fearlessly and finished with a huge sense of accomplishment.

THE END

Dorothy's Editorial Note: After reading Jeremy's account of our kayaking adventures, I could not help but notice how abruptly he concludes the section about the rapids. Let me fill in where he left off. At the first set of rapids, he was tossed from his ducky like a little rag doll. It then took two guides about five minutes to get him back into his boat. I found this amusing, as I never once fell out of my ducky. When we finished the ride, I told him that maybe these duckies were too dangerous for him, and I would buy him a little rubber ducky when we got home!

Author's Response: Dorothy's heavy drug use sometimes causes hallucinations. I apologize that she has interrupted your reading.

In the Lap of Luxury

✦

November 10, 2002
Rio de Janeiro, Brazil

I would like to take this opportunity to thank our unofficial corporate sponsor, Marriott Hotels. Prior to our trip, Dorothy and I worked as management consultants for five years on projects that required extensive business travel. During this time, we collectively accumulated enough Marriott Reward points to allow us twenty-seven free nights at various Marriott hotels around the world. The first of these stays was in the JW Marriott Copacabana Resort, right in the middle of Brazil's teeming beach culture. From our luxury beachfront abode, we planned to spend five days absorbing Rio's famed sun, restaurants, and festive nightlife.

Now, it is important to remember that we had been backpacking through South America for the past three months, staying almost exclusively in budget accommodations. One hostel we stayed in cost a staggering $2 per night. This included natural lighting (a window), an antique mattress (that was at least fifty years old), maid service (annually), and your own pet rat. I'm exaggerating of course. All residents had to share the rat.

One can only imagine the culture shock we faced when we arrived in the grand lobby of the Marriott in Rio de Janeiro. I will tell a story to help paint you a picture.

It started the night before in Santiago, Chile. That evening we went out with Antonio and Giovanna, a couple we knew through a mutual friend in New York. They were extremely gracious hosts and showed us a great time. Perhaps too good of a time. A couple of important details here. First, Chileans don't go to dinner until around 11:00 PM and would never dream of showing their face in a night-club until 2:00 AM. That put us in bed around 4:30 AM. Second, our flight to Rio was at 6:30 AM, so we had scheduled a cab to pick us up at 5:30 AM.

When the alarm went off at 5:00, we were in pain. I stumbled to the bathroom, shaved my teeth, sprayed deodorant in my hair, and peeled the beer bottle label from my forehead. We threw on whatever clothes we could find and quickly packed, haphazardly shoving random gear into the backpack. As we stumbled outside, our taxi was just pulling up.

After fighting to stay awake while battling the crowds at the airport, we finally made it to our seats on the airplane and crashed out for some much needed sleep. We landed in Rio invigorated from our rest and ready to check out our first nice hotel accommodation in months. We jumped in a taxi and were off to the Marriott.

Upon arrival, we immediately caught some strange looks from the valet staff. I started to feel a little self-conscious and took a closer examination of my clothes, baggage, and person. Everything seemed in good order. I mean there were a few little things, but nothing that would cause a scene at any of our previous hostels. For example:

- My hair had not been combed for three months

- I had not shaved in two weeks

- There was a "Tequila Rock" stamp on my left hand

- I was wearing camouflage cargo shorts that were filthy from hiking in southern Chile

- My slightly-stained T-shirt, which I had converted into a sleeveless V-neck with my pocket knife, proudly proclaimed, "Cerveza, It's Not Just for Breakfast Anymore"

- I exuded a slight odor that I had grown accustomed to about six weeks earlier

- I had on some really sweet shades that made me look like a 1970s porn star
- My backpack had a pair of dirty boxer shorts sticking out of one of the side pockets

Nothing too bad. And Dorothy looked positively stunning, as always, so I could see no problem.

A couple of bellboys came over and started loading our bags onto a luggage rack. I immediately protested. Having slummed it for about three months, I lived by one simple rule: The bags never left my sight unless they were under lock and key. The bell captain adamantly insisted that our bags would be safe in his care, but I was having none of it. Something about budget travel left me trusting no one. I even kept an eye on Dorothy.

We took the lobby by storm. I thought the concierge was going to faint. As we passed, I gave him a quick wink. "The rest of the band will be here in about an hour. Have our instruments stored in a safe place and send up the champagne immediately."

We made our way to the check-in desk. The reservation manager noticed us instantly. "I am sorry, but we have no vacancies. I can recommend a great hostel just up the road."

"Wrong answer," I replied. "My lovely wife and I are platinum level members." I slapped the joint Marriott Visa on the counter. "I believe you will find a reservation for one of your suites for the next five nights."

Slightly aghast, he checked the reservation, then quickly hailed a bellboy and handed over our keys. We were ushered along as quickly as they could manage.

This is where it gets good. Upon arriving in our room, we were all surprised to see that the linens had not been changed. The bellboy called the front desk. After a few minutes of intense Portuguese, he handed me the phone. It was the reservation manager. "I am very sorry about your room, Mr. Sonnenburg. There are no other normal suites currently available. I have therefore upgraded you to the presidential suite, with an ocean view. I will have the keys sent right up." I could hear the pain in his voice.

As we stood in our presidential suite, it took me a good ten minutes to remember the bellboy was hanging around for a tip. I handed him all the Chilean coins I could find. After he left, we changed into our bathing suits and headed towards the beach. On the way out, the concierge called to me, "Sir, what band did you say you were with?"

"The Stingrays," I replied. "When the rest the boys show up, tell them I have checked into the presidential suite and that I will see them at the beach. Oh, and the champagne, ice cold. Thanks."

Thanksgiving in Patagonia

✦

November 30, 2002
El Chalten, Argentina

Dorothy and I spent Thanksgiving hiking, glacier trekking, and ice climbing in Patagonia, an ice-capped frontier spanning the southern regions of Argentina and Chile. As many of our fellow Americans sat down to enjoy their Thanksgiving meals, we were just completing an exhaustive morning exploration of Argentina's Glacier National Park, a place we will always remember for its vast natural beauty and ever-present sense of remoteness. Our stomachs were growling with annual memories of turkey, gravy, and all the trimmings when the guide turned and told us, "OK, we rest here and you can eat the packed lunch you brought with you."

Packed lunch—a small but seemingly very important detail our guide forgot to mention when we signed-up for the trip. Dorothy and I exchanged a defeated glance. As I stood on the glacier, surrounded by florescent blue ice formations, I was reminded of the movie *Alive*. It is based on a true story about plane-wreck survivors who are forced to resort to cannibalism. If I recalled correctly, it was set in Patagonia. I looked over at our tour guide. He was a nice meaty man. His Grade-A muscles were marbled with just enough fat to cook up nice and juicy. Then I looked down at my ice-climbing ax, which I held in gloved hand. No fingerprints. Hell, no one out here to find him anyway. I caught Dorothy's attention, then darted my eyes back and forth between my ice ax and the guide while licking my lips.

As I amused Dorothy with fake hacking gestures to the back of his head[1], a couple from Missouri approached us. "If you did not pack a lunch, then you are more than welcome to share ours. It's not quite turkey and gravy, but there should be enough to go around. We can have our own little Thanksgiving dinner, right here on this glacier."

I was really touched. The American sense of Thanksgiving had reached beyond the homeland borders to find us at the farthest corner of the earth. I then remembered that they had witnessed my performance with my ice ax. I think they were a little nervous that after I ate the guide, we would not be able to find our way back to civilization. Then they would be next. "Ah shit, Marge. We are hiking through the wilderness with Hannibal Lector. Better share our cheese and crackers so he doesn't size us up for dessert."

After our little Thanksgiving feast, we set out to climb a seventy-five-foot vertical sheet of ice. Our guide explained that ice climbing is similar to climbing a ladder. "The trick is to let your legs do the work. Kick the front teeth of your steel crampons into the ice. Then reach up and drive the tip of the ax into the ice. Push yourself upward using your leg muscles. You should only hold onto the ice axes for balance."

While the guide's explanation was pretty good, it significantly underplayed the role of the ice ax. They should only be used for balance. Ha! Let's define balance. Balance is not falling off the side of that freakin' mountain and plummeting to your death on the icy spikes of the glacier below. All of the sudden, the ice ax seems of the utmost importance, doesn't it? You hang onto those ice axes for dear life. Every time I would try to kick the front spikes of my crampons into the ice, they would slip. I would face-plant into the wall with my feet dangling below me. And you know the one thought going through my head? "DON'T LET GO OF THE ICE AXES OR YOU WILL DIE!!!"

OK, I exaggerated a bit. The ice axes aren't the most important part of your climbing gear. That honor goes to your safety line. Even a strong, strapping

---

1.   It is scary what you find funny while starving in the frozen wilderness

Texas man can only hang onto the handles of those ice axes for so long before something gives. Either a glove slips, the ax comes free, or in most cases, your arms just give out. The first time this happened, a couple of distinct thoughts went through my head: "I'll never live long enough to make it to the nearest hospital," and "I hope the others don't eat my corpse!"

But after about five feet, the safety rope caught. The rope runs through a pulley at the top of the mountain and is controlled by the guide below. I heard him grunt, "Ay carumba, este hombre es muy pesado!." *(Damn, this guy is really heavy!)*

For the final fifteen feet of the ascent, I don't think I was climbing as much as being hoisted on the rope by the guide below. I was exhausted and used all my remaining energy to avoid another slip. In the end, I guess it was good I didn't eat the guide. My fat, frozen ass would still be sitting at the base of that ice wall if it weren't for his help.

I can reflect back on Patagonia as one of the most beautiful and exciting parts of our trip. But as for Thanksgiving, next year I will happily embrace turkey, college football, and an afternoon nap.

Fishing at the End of the World

✦

November 28, 2002
Ushuaia, Argentina

Dorothy and I first met Sibylle, a German woman about our age, on a twenty-six-hour bus ride from Rio de Janeiro to the Iguazu Falls. The three of us immediately bonded, based on our mutual need to complain about the difficulties and discomforts of budget travel. At the time, our conversations mainly focused on long-distance bus trips.[1] We traveled together for the next three days and then remained in contact via email. Through this correspondence, we realized our paths would cross again in Ushuaia, Argentina, so we made plans to stay at the same hostel and explore the region together.

Dorothy and I had now been traveling for three months, spending every waking minute together. We took the same tours, saw the same sights, met the same

---

1. A twenty-six-hour bus ride in Brazil is almost as much fun as spending twenty-six hours grating your elbow across coarse concrete.

people, and read the same books. Our only time apart was to go to the bathroom (not exactly a period for inner reflection given the condition of the toilets we had encountered). It is probably fair to say our spousal-annoyance factor was quite high. Upon arriving at the hostel to meet Sibylle, we were both feeling particularly irritable. Within the first hour of our group reunion, Dorothy and I had several minor blow-ups about such petty things as:

- Walking at incorrect speeds
- Choosing the wrong seats on the bus
- Packing the suntan lotion in the side pocket instead of the front pocket
- Not knowing the Spanish word for "constipated"
- Taking too long to decide on a dish at dinner
- Winking at a flirtatious eighteen-year-old Argentinean girl (just kidding, Dorothy would never do that)

Finally, Sibylle had enough and decided Dorothy and I needed a day apart. She determined that when we woke up in the morning, she would take Dorothy hiking for the day, and I would be left to fend for myself. We politely protested for 1.7 seconds, and then happily agreed.

Ushuaia is located in the very southern tip of Patagonia, and has been dubbed "El Fin del Mundo" (*The End of the World*). It is well-known amongst anglers for its great trout fly-fishing. For those of you who don't know much about fishing, let me take a brief moment to introduce you to the sport. There are two extreme ends of the spectrum: deep-sea fishing and fly-fishing. I use to live on the Gulf of Mexico and went deep-sea fishing several times. I didn't have my own boat, so I would always get together with a group of buddies and charter a cruiser, captain, and crew. On these trips, we'd kick back and soak up the sun while a couple of deckhands rigged up tackle that could easily hoist the Titanic. The rods were as strong as a crane, the fishing line was effectively steel cable, and the hooks looked like modern-day decedents of medieval weapons. Then the boat would troll around trying to tempt *Jaws* to bite. Once a fish went for the bait, we'd strap ourselves into a chair and smile like champs as we reeled in our prize. It was a huge payoff that required minimal expertise on my part.

And then there is fly-fishing. I knew (and still know) very little about fly-fishing. But how different could it be from deep-sea fishing, right? So I wasted no time in tracking down a fishing guide and arranging a fly-fishing trip for my day away from my better half.

Right from the start, things did not go well. Casting a fly-fishing rod is something of an art, requiring the fisherman to swing the fly back and forth overhead while slowly releasing more line. I had never done this before. My first attempt almost hooked my guide's eyebrow. My second attempt landed me in the bushes, twenty feet behind us. I became something of a spectacle. Everyone cleared the bank for 100 feet on either side of me. Old men were gathered together, smoking cigarettes, pointing, and cracking up at each failed attempt. Little kids were in a circle placing bets. A couple of teenagers screamed phrases of encouragement which probably translated into, "Hey, gringo, you'd have better luck jumping in the lake and catching a fish with your hands." My guide looked embarrassed. He would come over and explain the technique to me in Spanish and then run down the bank for cover before I tried again. I was hopeless. At one point, the fly landed in the water about five feet from the bank. Everybody cheered.

Finally, the guide decided to try a different tack. We jumped in the car and headed to a small creek. This time he brought out the easy-to-cast push-button-release reel, the fishing equivalent of training wheels, and announced that we would abandon fly-fishing and try with lures. I had fished with lures before and gave a sigh of relief.

On my previous fishing trips, I was casting into the ocean. The idea was simple—cast as far as possible. This stream was very different. It was maybe six feet wide. There were numerous trees with low hanging branches along the creek. The water was an obstacle course of submerged logs, rocks, and tree roots. Casting here was about precision, not distance.

As we set up our rods, the guide pointed out places along the creek where trout were known to congregate. He advised, "Cast down steam, under the branches but over the log, to the left of the rock but not too close to the tree roots along the bank on the right."

"No problem," I replied. To no surprise, my first cast went right into the tree branches. He shook his head. After trying for five minutes to get the lure free, we finally cut the line. He tied on another lure and we headed down the creek to a place with fewer trees.

I spent the next thirty minutes casting onto the opposite bank, into the tree roots, and on top of logs, but lost no more lures (which had become my new yardstick for success). My guide saw that I seemed to be holding my own, and he moved a bit further down the creek to try a different area. Then the inevitable occurred: I was hung up in the trees again. I spent several minutes trying to get the lure free, dreading having to face the guide again. I tried tugging the line from different angles, giving it fierce shakes, and even climbing out to it, but all to no avail.

I was about to give up but decided to give it one final tug. SNAP! The pole broke straight in half. I couldn't believe it. My guide had just rounded the creek bend, with a fish in hand, to witness the trauma. His jaw dropped as he stared in disbelief.

He did not let me cast the rest of the afternoon. He would cast and then hand me the pole like I was a child. I was humiliated.

The only solace was that he did catch a very nice trout, which I claimed as my own later that evening as I showed it off to Dorothy and Sibylle. I then presented both of them a gift, matching walking sticks (which were joined together as a fishing pole in a previous life). We cooked the fish for dinner and sat down to eat and discuss our day apart. I omitted only a few small details.

Caving and Other Jetlagged Adventures

✦

December 8, 2002
Waitomo Caves, New Zealand

A few days after my fishing trip in Ushuaia, we left Buenos Aires on a short little flight around the world to Auckland, New Zealand. Our flight departed Argentina at 6:25 PM on December 4th and, given the length of the flight, layovers, and the time change, did not arrive in New Zealand until 4:25 AM on December 6th. We had a reservation to pick up a campervan at 7:00 that morning.

You want some good travel advice? If you ever take a flight that lands a full two days after it departs, don't plan to operate any sort of heavy machinery for a month. I wouldn't even recommend attempting conversation for a week. When we showed up at the rental agency, I was so jetlagged I could hardly function. The agent greeted us with a warm smile. "Did you have a nice flight?"

I glanced over to Dorothy for help. She was slumped in her chair, head spasmodically bobbing as she faded in and out of consciousness, mumbling incoherently. I returned my blank gaze back to the agent, finally managing a weak smile that caused a bit of drool to drip from the corner of my mouth.

"OK, then. Sir, can I see your driver's license?"

My wallet weighed a ton, causing me to make a little grunting sound as I hoisted it from my pocket. Opening it was a struggle, as I had the dexterity and eye-hand coordination of a two-year-old. Credit cards, legal documents, pictures, and NZ currency all blurred in a mass of confusion. One card fell out on the table. Relieved, I pushed it over to her.

"Um, sir, this is your Blockbuster video card."

"Sorry," I heard some distant voice say. I handed her my entire wallet and then rested my head in my hands.

She stared at the wallet awkwardly for a minute and then opened it and found my license. "OK, sir, do you want to take any additional insurance."

I pondered this without lifting my head or opening my eyes. "Just auto insurance," a disembodied voice replied.

She sighed with frustration. "And will there be any additional drivers."

Just give me the damn keys, lady. I am dying here! I opened my eyes and shot her a look to show her that I was losing my patience. "I imagine, but I plan to avoid crowded places. Plus, aren't the other drivers required to have their own insurance."

"Uh huh," she paused for a second to consider the possibility that she was dealing with a lunatic. "I meant other drivers for your vehicle, sir, but I'll take that as a no." She shook her head in defeat. "Here are your keys. You might think about pulling over for a rest before you drive too far."

And we were off. Now, besides sleep deprivation, there was an additional factor working against me as we pulled out of the parking lot. Consider this: in the States, when you take a right turn, you do not have to cross traffic, and therefore only need to check the traffic coming from your left. A quick diagram to illustrate this point:

American Right Turn

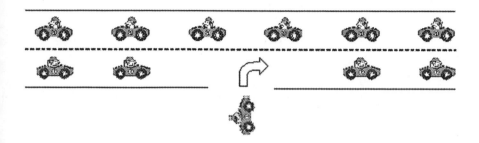

In New Zealand (or any other country which chooses to drive on the wrong side of the road), when you take a right, you must cross the near lane of traffic (which is coming from the right) and turn into the far lane. Here is a diagram to illustrate how this looks to a jetlagged American who instinctively only checks traffic coming from the left:

Jetlagged American Turning Right in New Zealand

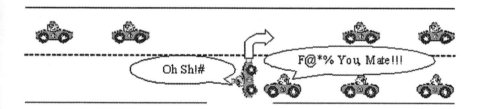

This managed to wake me up. In fact, I suddenly felt like I just had just drunk three pots of coffee, dumped cold water on my head, and then taken a leak on a live wire. Dorothy also sprang into action. "What was that?"

"Nothing, honey," I replied. "Just a little turbulence. Try to go back to sleep." She was asleep before I had finished my sentence.

Fully awake, it was now painfully clear to me that I was in no condition to drive[1]. I checked us into the closest campervan park I could find. This happened to be the parking lot of the supermarket right down the block. I pulled into a nice shaded spot, locked the doors, climbed into the back, and crashed.

---

1. Because I didn't know what country I was in or how I had obtained this nice campervan.

2 hours later...

KNOCK-KNOCK-KNOCK. "Hey, is anyone in there." I peered through the curtains. I had attracted the attention of the local authorities. Very local that is. Mr. Security Guard looked like he wanted some answers. He had readied his walkie-talkie, apparently to call in back-up (I guess the grocery store clerks) if the situation turned ugly.

"Yeah, someone is in here." I opened the side door. "Can I help you?"

"We don't allow people to just sleep in the parking lot. It is reserved for customers."

"Right. Well, I was in there making my shopping list." I ripped out a page from Dorothy's journal. "There, now I am all finished."

"Oh, sorry sir. Have a nice day." He retreated to his post on the sidewalk, ready to pounce if we returned to snooze city.

Not wanting to blow my cover, I woke up Dorothy and we headed into the store. We strolled the aisles and selected a few of your essential road-trip items: beef jerky, Gatorade, Best of the 70s 5-disc box set compilation, and a *Cosmopolitan* magazine (for Dorothy of course. I don't ever read that stuff...well, at least not while I am driving).

Two hours later, we arrived at the Waitomo Caves, where we had signed-up to go on *The Lost World Epic* tour, recently featured in *The Amazing Race*. This eight-hour tour is not for the squeamish. It starts with a 330-foot abseil (or repel, as it is more commonly known in North America) down into the Waitomo Cave system. This is the longest commercial rope-controlled descent of its kind in the world. Once in the cave, the rest of the day is spent running, jumping, swimming, wading, climbing, sliding, and crawling through the maze of underground rivers and caves. The trip concludes by sitting in the darkness, staring at the cave ceiling, which is covered with thousands of glow worms. The brochure claimed they looked like stars from a distant galaxy.

That next morning, we met Rusty, the guide who was to lead our fearless group. I need to take a brief moment here to introduce the New Zealand culture for those who have not been to this incredible, yet remote country. Don't worry friends, I am not about to veer off on a history lesson, talk about value systems, or lay out their political framework (mainly because I don't know about any of this). No, I can sum up the entire essence of what it means to be a Kiwi in only two words: *adrenaline junkies*. They speak of skydiving and bungee jumping with the same casualness that we would discuss rollerblading and surfing the net.

Within the first hour of talking to Rusty, he told two stories worth sharing. The first is about how he spends his free time. "Yeah, I have gone bungee jumping like twenty-three times and skydiving almost thirty. I don't even like it anymore because I don't get a rush. I mean, with all the safety equipment they make you wear, you know that nothing is going to go wrong. Lately, my buddies and I are into a new sport we kind of invented, called bridge jumping. Basically, you tie one end of a rope to a point in the center of the bridge. Then you walk down to one end of the bridge and clip onto the line, taking out all the slack. Then we jump off. It swings you like a pendulum, back and forth. It is a lot better than bungee jumping because you have to do all your own rope work and measurements, so something could always go wrong! It is a ripper."

A ripper. I am sure it is.

The second story was about his youth. "So one time I am playing rugby, and this huge dude tackles me from the side. When we landed, his knee came right down on my ear. I got up and I could not hear a thing. I checked myself out and found that I was just bleeding from my ear. Nothing serious, so I kept playing. Later that night, I am at a party hitting on these girls and I start smoking a cigarette. They all just stare at me and one of them says, 'Oh my god, the smoke's coming out of your ear!' How cool is that? They loved it. Unfortunately, it only worked that one night. I still can't hear real well out of that ear."

Imagine that. I thought about explaining the modern invention of a helmet; however, I am glad I didn't. Nothing seems to give Kiwis more pleasure than to make fun of American football players for wearing helmets and padding. "Rugby is a man's sport. No helmets. No padding. Hell, you have to be tough to play rugby," they would say as their heads made slight involuntary twitches caused by one too many concussions.

And this was the guy whom we would trust with our lives as he rigged us up for the mammoth descent? For those who aren't experienced mountaineers or cavers (much like yours truly), the idea of abseiling is to use friction to enable you to slide down a rope in a controlled manner. You start by strapping into a harness. This device has one stirrup for each leg, a belt around your waist, and a metal ring in the front made for attaching snaps, clamps, buckles, and other accessories. (Sounds like some sort of S&M device, doesn't it?) A little metal contraption named a "figure eight" is attached to the front ring in your harness and the rope you plan to descend is fed through it. With your dominant hand, you control the descent rope. If you pull the rope down, the friction applied by the figure eight will cause you to stop, hanging in mid-air. If you ease the tension, you slide down the rope. If you let go of the rope, you plummet to your death. I am sure I have missed some things here, but this is the basic idea. Or at least that is the theory as Rusty described it.

Three hundred and thirty feet is a long way down. We peered down into the cavern and could not see the bottom. Then came the hardest part, starting the descent. Technically, it is quite a simple maneuver. Turn away from the edge and step backwards over the side into the abyss. If Rusty's explanations about friction are correct, you should just hang there. Otherwise, well, have you ever seen Wylie Coyote in the Roadrunner cartoon? I think you get the idea.

And so we took the leap of faith, one at a time. The laws of physics prevailed, and we slowly enjoyed a spectacular descent lasting about twenty minutes. Upon arriving at the bottom, we took a moment to appreciate our surroundings. Earlier explorers described this deep mouth of the cave as a "fairytale land." It is quite fitting. Rays of light beamed down through the chamber to illuminate the mist rising off the underground river. Wild ferns grew along the banks and large boulders were scattered about. Standing here, it was easy to see why *The Lord of the Rings* was filmed in New Zealand.

We turned on our headlamps and ascended a short path leading into the next cavern. There we met the underground river and spent the next couple of hours wading and swimming our way from one underground cave to the next. It was incredible.

After a short break for tea and coffee, we branched away from the river onto a path deeper into the cave complex. I was at the front of the group and noticed that up ahead the cave narrowed into what appeared to be an impasse. Rusty patted me on the back and pointed to a small opening underneath one of the boulders. "Under there, mate," he instructed. I froze. The space was probably eighteen inches high and twenty-four inches wide. I have a bad case of claustrophobia, I think because my parents used to punish me by locking me in a coffin when I was a child (just kidding). I have just always hated tight spaces. As I started to protest, Rusty stood firm, "Look, mate, there are girls in the group behind you who are ready to go. Besides, what else do you propose? Do want to hike back to that 330-foot rope and try to climb it?"

Reputation was on the line, so I got down on my hands and knees and started moving into the space. Before I even got my head in, I realized that I was not going to be able to crawl, so I flattened onto my belly and attempted to slither in like a snake. I was barely able to use my elbows and feet to continue pushing me forward. Like most Texan men, I have broad shoulders and a shapely beer gut, neither of which were helping the situation. Several times I got stuck and had to squirm backwards to readjust my position while attempting to fight off panic. I was about eight feet into the narrow tunnel before I heard Dorothy's voice behind me. "Look, I am not going into that small tunnel. The tour brochure said nothing about having to squirm through tight spaces." The others in the group agreed with noticeable hostility.

There was a pause and then Rusty answered, "Well, if none of you guys want to squirm through that small tunnel, I guess we can just walk through this little passage on my right and meet Jeremy on the other side." Everyone erupted in laughter.

THAT BASTARD!!!

I could now hear the group about six feet in front of me.

"Come on, Jeremy. We are all waiting for you."

"Looks like a tight fit in there. You need some Vaseline?"

"Wishing you hadn't had three sandwiches for lunch, aren't you big fella?"

Yep, everyone had become a comedian. My blood boiled as I continue to work my way through the tight passage. Finally, my head emerged into a large opening and I heard another eruption of laughter and clapping. Dorothy helped me up and gave me a big hug. Rusty was particularly pleased with himself. "You should have seen your face, man. I thought you were going to cry." HA-HA-HA.

We finally came to the last cavern, featuring thousands of glow worms. We turned off our headlamps and sat down to contemplate the florescent green glow of these strange little creatures. It felt extraterrestrial. It was a moment for reflection. I spent the time questioning some of the deeper meanings of life, staring with awe into a universe of subterranean heavenly bodies. After fifteen minutes, we came back to earth as Rusty relit his headlamp. As we continued on the path towards the exit of the cave, Dorothy asked Rusty, "What makes them glow?"

"Well, those little worms don't actually produce any excrement. Instead they have an internal chemical reaction which basically burns off any extra energy. Simply put, we were sitting there staring at little glowing pieces of shit."

Nicely put, Rusty. Nicely put. Glad to see I had been so inspired by something of such magnitude and greatness. I will close by saying this adventure was by far the most unique and unearthly experience I have ever had. And that goes for the whole adventure, not just the reflective contemplation of glowing worm shit.

Intro to Wine Tasting

✦

December 12, 2002
Marlborough Wine Region, New Zealand

I have always preferred beer to wine. This is not to say I never drink wine, but given the choice I am going to order a Bud over a Chardonnay ten times out of ten. Sure, I understand the wine basics. Wine can be split into two different types. Traditional wine, which is made from grapes and is either red or white in color, and wine coolers, which come in any color you want and are made by spiking Gatorade. I prefer the traditional stuff, since I am a pretty classy guy, and I usually keep a box of it in my fridge.

Marlborough, New Zealand, is one of the fastest-growing wine regions in the world. Dorothy and I had never been to a wine-tasting before, but we were both eager to give it a try. Our tour started at Montana, the region's largest and most popular vineyard. I was expecting a modest, quaint little operation sitting on a couple of acres of land, where the children would be out picking grapes while mom and pop ran the winery and the little visitor center. Hardly. After a quick guided walk of the facilities, I found my expectations couldn't have been further from the truth. There were grape vines as far as the eye could see. Immaculate polished-chrome harvesting machines, forklifts, and eighteen-wheelers lined the loading bays. The visitor center featured a trendy wine bar, high-end gift store, chic restaurant, plasma TVs, and stylish leather couches. The warehouse where the wine was fermented and aged looked like a hi-tech laboratory, with the exception of the thousands of French oak casks. Montana viewed wine making as a delicate balance of art, science, tradition, and technology. And they took it quite seriously.

As we concluded the walk, I followed the group to the bar for a wine tasting. Our group leader started by showing us the proper technique for tasting wine:

1. **Look at the wine:**

   She made an elaborate demonstration and held her glass up, tilting it as far over as possible. "Now what do you notice?" she asked the group.

   "That you didn't pour me very much," I thought to myself. Some others in the group, who were more experienced wine tasters, rambled on about the color, clarity, legs, etc. I was clearly out of my league, so I added, "It's so beautiful." This seemed to get several nods, so I was quite proud of myself.

2. **Smell the wine:**

   Another huge ordeal. She enthusiastically swirled the wine in her glass, apparently to get as much oxygen to the wine as possible, and then stuck her nose right into the glass. We all did the same. "Now, what can you smell?" This time she was staring directly at me.

   I should have kept my mouth shut earlier. I thought I'd better go for a joke. "Grapes!" One slight snicker from an English guy, obviously another beer drinker, and twenty cold stares which seemed to say, "You are a complete idiot."

   "No, not grapes," she responded, as if she were embarrassed for me. "There are hints of mango, lime, pineapple, and gooseberry."

   My ass. What the hell does gooseberry smell like anyway?

I thought I would just let it go, but she was quite passionate about this. She grabbed another glass and handed it to me, "Now here, swirl this one around, inhale deeply and tell me what you smell."

I picked the glass up, gave it a huge swirl, closed my eyes, and took a huge sniff. "Green apples, honey, baby's breath, and a hint of ripe doozleberry," I said in a warm, poetic voice. I opened my eyes.

She was all smiles. "That was fantastic!!! Very well done."

Others were almost fighting over the glass to see if they could pick up the same scents. Dorothy whispered into my ear, "Doozleberry?"

I winked at her and replied, "I made it up, I think."

3. **Taste the wine.**

Finally. I mean I didn't come on the tour to smell fruit. However, there was a correct way to do this as well. Take a bit in your mouth, swirl it around, and then suck in a little air (again, to get more oxygen into the wine). I tried this once, instantly choked, and almost spit wine all over Dorothy. Not cool. The rest of the time, I did it the old fashion way. Down the hatch.

Despite all the sarcasm, I was having a really good time. By the fourth winery we visited, I was having a *great* time. At each winery we tried seven to ten different types of wines—you do the math. Riesling, Rosé, Sauvignon Blanc, Pinot Noir, Merlot, Cabernet, Shiraz, Port, Rudy-Tudy-Fresh-N-Fruity—we tried them all. And the best part: the tastings were free.

By this time I had become pretty good buddies with the English guy who had laughed at my joke earlier. The two of us had devised a little game where we would try to come up with the funniest comments to write in the wineries guest book.

His best was, "A friendly place with cheap drink prices, but they are a little light on the pour. Could stand to have a better selection of beers and should consider adding a pool table."

My best was, "Rosé, a tasty little number with shapely legs, an innocent pink complexion, and a lingering sweet aftertaste. I plan to let her mature another couple of years and then take her out to my summer home and enjoy her in the lush green grass of the meadows, the soft fine sand on the beaches, and at night in the hot tub." I signed it, "Rusty, from Waitomo."

After the last winery, which was either number six or sixteen, we piled back in the bus and headed back to our campsite. I am now considerably more knowledgeable about wines, but I think I will still stick with my friend, Bud.

Bridge Climbing

✦

January 1, 2003
Sydney, Australia

During the Great Depression, Sydney, Australia, faced surging unemployment. The masses called upon the government to step in and save the city from grave despair. The politicians rose to the challenge and proposed an idea so bold and forward thinking that eighty years later it was still appreciated by millions when Sydney kicked off worldwide New Year's Eve celebrations. These visionaries planned to put the people to work building the largest firework launch pad the world had ever seen. Sixteen hundred of Sydney's finest would unite to erect over 50,000 tons of steel, flares, and explosives in the shape of a 1,650-foot coat hanger across Sydney Harbor. Even Paul Hogan (Crocodile Dundee) pitched in and helped out as a painter[1]. Original plans were later modified by bureaucratic pragmatists, who scrapped a massive disco ball and spinning concert stage to

---

1.   True, albeit a little later

make room for pedestrian, rail, and automotive crossings. Yet despite these challenges and ulterior motives, the original pioneers persevered, and in1932 the pyrotechnics masterpiece was completed. And that, my friends, is the story of Sydney Harbor Bridge…or at least my version of the story.

Now, here is the forward-thinking bit. These guys knew that if they were to build such a massive structure, rising some 450 feet in height, their great-grandchildren would naturally have the urge to climb it. So the original design was engineered to allow any able-bodied adventurer to climb to the top of the arch with relative ease and safety. Today, this might seem like a bit of a no-brainer, but back then, it was foresight. Maybe even genius.

Lo and behold, in 1998, BridgeClimb opened for business, leading guided tours to the top of the arch. And being the able-bodied adventurers we are, Dorothy and I decided to give it a go. We even managed to talk a friend of ours, Jason, into joining us. Dorothy and I first met Jason about two years ago, when all three of us were working as consultants in London. During evenings and weekends, Jason was part of the Australian drinking-militia which had invaded London and established a stronghold near the Earl's Court tube station. For several years, the British forces have been trying to retake the Earl's Court area, but the Australians are deeply rooted in the local pubs, hostels, and late-night kebab shops. By the time the British caught up with Jason and kicked him out of the country, his Aussie beer soldiers were about fifteen million strong and growing. Anyway, Jason had flown from Melbourne to join us for a little New Year's Eve celebration. Oh, and Jason does not like heights.

Australians are quite a festive group, not only in London but in their home country as well. And this is not just a casual observation. Check this out. When we arrived at the BridgeClimb offices, we started filling out all the standard paperwork. As with most of these sorts of activities, one of the standard terms and conditions stated that you could not be under the influence of alcohol. To ensure this, each climber would be given a breath test. Just insurance wording, I thought. Wrong. Our climbing guide actually lined us up and had each of us blow into a little contraption that determined our blood-alcohol level. I found it quite amusing that drunken climbing was such a concern that the company had resorted to a pre-climb sobriety test. Even better, I was sitting next to these two Aussie guys and overheard the following conversation:

"Oh, mate. I am a little concerned about this breath test."

"Yeah, me too."

"Well at least we haven't had anything to drink today."

"Yeah, but last night was massive. I think I might still be drunk."

Now, here is the kicker. It was 9:30 PM. Must have been some party. I watched as the first one blew. "You passed," proclaimed the guide.

"Nice one!" his friend congratulated. Then he blew.

"Well, doesn't look like you are going to be able to climb, mate." The guide gave him a stern look as the guy turned pale. There was no refund policy, so he would be out the cash. Plus, he was incredibly embarrassed. Then, the guide smiled. "No, I'm just kidding. You're fine." The crowd erupted in laughter.

"True? Oh, mate. That was a shocker. Good onya," he laughed.

The trip starts with a walk underneath the main motorway of the bridge. After about 400 feet, we came to a set of ladders. It turned out there were four consecutive ladders, each about fifty-five feet high. To make things even more interesting, these ladders were in the middle of six lanes of traffic.[2] As soon as I started to climb, I was momentarily blinded by oncoming traffic, like an animal frozen in headlights. All I could hear was engines gunning, horns honking, and tires screeching. Ravenous vehicular wolves, hungry to devour my remains if I were to lose my grip. I climbed one slow, steady step at a time until finally I was above the fury of the automotive predators below. My vision returned, I took a nice look around, and I thought out loud, "What am I doing?"

Jason was in ear shot and responded, "I don't know, but this is the stupidest thing I have ever let you talk me into. We could be in a pub, having a beer and appreciating the view of the bridge from a barstool like normal people."

I looked down at him. There was no color in his face. His fear of heights was apparently raging. "Don't worry, mate," I consoled with a smirk. "We are almost a quarter of the way up. Not much further now. And once we get up there, we can turn around, climb down again, and then go to a pub. Shouldn't take much more than about an hour and a half. Less if you slip on the way down."

"Sonnenburg, I find this whole experience about as enjoyable as a pimple on my ass," he sneered.

"You two just pay attention to what you're doing," Dorothy reprimanded.

"Yes, Mom," we replied in unison.

Once we conquered the ladders, it was a short, easy walk up the arch to the summit.

It was a very relaxed and enjoyable experience for most of us. Then there was Jason. I'd seen him better. He was clearly shaken. "Sonnenburg, this is absolutely

---

2.   Or possibly sixty lanes of traffic. Despite my unflinching commitment to journalistic accuracy, at the time I was predisposed with hanging onto the railing for dear life and wondering if my life-insurance policy covered accidental death while climbing celebratory rocket-launching structures.

the worst. In fact, I would rank it right up there with full-body searches, sunburned genitalia, and last call."

I cracked up. He continued his angry ranting, but I couldn't hear it over my own laughter. We finally arrived at the top and stood silently, appreciating the splendid view of the Sydney Opera House. Even Jason managed a weak smile. We stayed there for about ten minutes as our guide told us several interesting and amusing stories. Here is my favorite:

Several years ago, before the bridge was open to commercial climbers, a maintenance engineer found a shopping cart on the top of the arch. Inside the cart were 126 empty VB (Victoria Bitter) beer cans. Now, think back on the climb I just described. Can you imagine the effort and dedication that would be required to get a shopping cart loaded with 126 cans of beer up four fifty-five-foot ladders? Even if you can conceive of how they physically accomplished the feat, how do you suppose they pulled it off without getting caught? Remember, the ladders are smack in the middle of traffic. A group of strapping young men heaving a shopping cart full of booze up a ladder is rather conspicuous, don't you think? I pondered this as we headed back down the ladders with traffic zipping by. You know what I concluded? People had to see them; they just didn't get reported to the cops. Or maybe, based on my impressions of the few Australians I have met so far, people actually slowed their cars and screamed encouragements.

"Good onya, boys. Looks like my kind of party."

"Nice one, blokes! Get bored of drinking in the pub, did ya?"

"You wee beauty. That is a good effort. You guys need a hand? I got some rope in the back seat."

I bet traffic came to a stop and the city united once again. This time, not to build the world's largest firework launch pad, but rather to support their countrymen in the ultimate pursuit of a rowdy evening.

It is the Australian way.

Tan Society

✦

January 5, 2003
Byron Bay, Australia

In Sydney, Dorothy and I rented a car and headed up the east coast en route to Cairns. We started with a slight detour to the Blue Mountains and then continued north, with stopovers in Newcastle and Bellingen. Finally, we arrived in Byron Bay, where we planned to stay a week.

Byron Bay is an eclectic mix of hippies, surfers, supermodels, backpackers, musicians, tattoo artists, vegetarians, wayward wanderers, bead jewelers, body-piercing specialists, university students, and one married couple (us). It boasts postcard-quality beaches with soft, golden sand and crystal blue water and is fondly renowned among Australians for its active nightlife.

For the most part, this is a community which prides itself on tolerance and individuality. However, after spending a couple of days here, I am sad to report a slight hypocrisy—a case of prejudice and discrimination. Namely, a mild contempt for anyone with the audacity to reveal untanned, pasty-white flesh. To show so much as a thigh that is not adequately golden-brown is met by stares, gasps, and comments like, "Dude, show some decency. Get some sun on that thing." Toned, tanned flesh is preferred, but flabby rolls are accepted, as long as they are properly bronzed. Eager to fit in with the sun-kissed masses, we checked into our hostel and got our ghostly pale bodies down to the beach.

Topless bathing is very popular in Australia, and nowhere is this more evident than Byron Bay. I personally think this is a very good thing. No, not because I am some pervert who gets excited by thousands of scantly clad women rubbing suntan lotion all over their breasts. For me, topless bathing is about gender equality, women's rights, and civil liberties. A woman should be allowed to tan her breasts with the same freedom as I choose to tan my beer gut. These women courageously bare themselves for freedom, for justice, and to protect their inalienable rights. I can personally think of no more noble a sight than a beach of breasts patriotically glistening in tropical oils. When Dorothy and I first arrived down at the beach, I was awestruck by this selfless act of humanity and righteously blubbered, "Oh, wow. Where's the camera? The guys back home are never going to believe this."

Dorothy, whose mind was in the gutter, failed to connect with this experience on my higher, more intellectual level, and slapped me on the back of the head several times. "Jeremy, if I catch you gawking at one more topless woman, then I am going to go topless myself."

"NO!!! Baby, you don't know how many perverts there are out here who get really excited by seeing topless woman lathering themselves up in suntan lotion. Not every guy has the same enlightened view on this issue as I do."

"Fine, but I am warning you, just one more time."

This was enough to scare me into discretion. Me staring at thousands of topless babes = GOOD. Thousands of tan, toned surfers staring at my topless wife = BAD. So, I continued across the beach, trying to look where I was walking but not focus specifically on any bared breasts.

Darkened sun junkies claimed most of the nice parts of the beach, leaving small cordoned-off areas near the grass for those of us who had previously lived among the shadows. Any attempt to settle in a sunbathing area of a higher tanning social class was met with hostile glares seeming to say, "Seats taken!" We finally made our way to an area of other SPF-500,000 users, laid out our towels, and began our ascent through the strata of beach society. After a couple of hours, we achieved a warm, tropical glow. Nothing like the deep, chocolate tans of the locals, but enough color to avoid being ostracized. We strolled back across the beach, still not focusing on any bare breasts, and headed back to our hostel.

That evening, we decided to check out Byron's famous nightlife. We headed to a bar aptly named "The Cheeky Monkey." There was a doorman out front. "OK, tanned people step right up. White pasties join the large line around back." We flashed our newly obtained olive-brown complexions and were immediately granted entrance. It was like school had just let out for summer. Cocktails were served in fishbowl-size glasses, the Beastie Boys were pumping out of the sound system, and sun-ripened travelers in their late teens and early twenties were dancing on the tables. A few pasties sat over in the corner by themselves. (Losers.) "Go get some rays, you sun virgins," the crowd taunted.

We were having a great time hanging out with our new tanned friends. Everyone was shaking their booty to timeless classics such as "Ice Ice Baby," "Dancing Queen," and "Greased Lightening." Then, the music stopped, and the DJ announced that the first person to bring him a matching pair of bra and panties would receive a free pitcher of beer. A pretty good offer, I thought. I asked Dorothy if I could borrow hers (ha). No, seriously, I was touched that such a rowdy place would pause to conduct a clothing drive for charity. Dorothy, whose mind was still in the gutter, again viewed the matter slightly differently. Regardless, the cause was successful, and the DJ collected one matching pair of female undergarments that proudly bore a print of the Union Jack. Just what some poor lady will need in her times of hardship. I am sure the Queen would be pleased.

And that is about the point where this old married couple figured it was probably best to head home (more Dorothy's decision than mine). So in conclusion, I would highly recommend a trip to Byron Bay, just probably not as a honeymoon destination! If you ever do head this direction, a bit of advice. Show up with a tan, wear dark sunglasses to the beach so no one can see your eyes, and carry matching lingerie in your pocket. You never know when it could be good for a free pitcher of beer.

The Quest of the Mighty Smurfs

✦

January 11, 2003
Fraser Island, Australia

Fraser Island is the largest all-sand island in the world. This stunning paradise, which is located just off Australia's eastern coast, possesses tropical terrain at its best. Lush rainforest surrounds freshwater lakes, shallow creeks, rolling sand dunes, champagne lagoons, and endless beaches. The island and its shoreline are also home to an exquisite array of wildlife. Dingoes roam the rugged wilderness while sharks, stingrays, whales, and dolphins can be spotted offshore from the island's many fine vantage points. It is a nature lover's dream.

Dorothy and I tend to prefer independent travel. I often find tour groups slightly annoying, a bit intrusive, and too well-organized for my liking. That said, it is often very difficult to strike out on an independent wilderness excursion while traveling. Sure, it can be done, but it requires the right gear, preparation, and experience. Nature can be fatally unforgiving otherwise. Gear costs money, preparation means lead time, and experience is inevitably lacking when trying new things. Therefore, when we set off on an expedition, we usually opt for a package which includes logistical support and local expertise. However, while guides help to ensure a safe trip, they usually also manage to eliminate much of the unexpected and, in turn, some of the fun. Damned if you do and possibly dead if you don't—such is the dilemma of an amateur adventurer.

The beauty of Fraser Island is that local tour companies understand this dilemma and have responded by offering self-drive island safaris. Independent travelers are pooled together into a group of nine to split the cost of equipment and provisions. The day before the trip, the group sits through two hours of briefings that explain the layout of the island, how to drive the truck, and things to watch out for. Then, they are turned loose with just enough knowledge to experience the fun of the unexpected without getting into any real trouble. On any given day, hundreds of these off-road novices come to the island to burn out clutches, overheat engines, and strip gearshifts. Who could pass up an opportunity for such chaos and mayhem? And, as an added bonus, everyone in the group received a delightfully tacky blue T-shirt with the logo of the tour company on the back. I immediately cut off the sleeves of mine and created a V-neck, as I do with all free T-shirts.

We had a good group. I will make introductions by tents. In the first tent was Sheila, a young Canadian woman making her way down the east coast to Sydney, where she was to meet up with some friends. Next, there was a Swedish couple, Boel and Martin. She looked like a model, he like a rock star. Then, there were Ann-Marie and Graeme, a couple from England. Both were easy-going, fun, and always good for a laugh. Finally, there were Neil and Melvyn, also from England. They were quick to point out that they were not a couple. Rather, they were sharing a tent because all the couples were already paired off and Sheila had politely refused both their offers as tent buddies.

At the conclusion of our briefing, the group was tasked with buying food for the trip. Martin, the Swedish rock star, suggested that it would be a great bonding opportunity for Graeme and me to do the shopping while the rest of the group headed to the local pub. Graeme and I exchanged grimaces, but before either of us could object, Martin had rallied the crowd and headed across the street. Stuck with no alternatives, we shrugged our shoulders and boarded the local taxi shuttle heading to the grocery store. Other self-drive groups were on the same shuttle and were reviewing their group shopping list. We felt slightly unprepared and decided a little planning was in order. We started the list where any Brit and Texan would. "So how much beer do you think we will need?" I asked.

"Blimey, I don't know. Shitloads. Better to buy too much than not enough. Worst scenario imaginable is to be stranded on that deserted island and run out of beer."

"Yeah. Plus, I imagine Martin would kill us."

"He might not get any. Running to the pub while sending us shopping. How cheeky can you get?"

"True. Well, let's just do the math on the beer. We will be out there two nights, we have nine people, and we will probably drink about five or six beers a night?"

"Five or six? Mate, have you lost your mind? Bullocks! Do you feel how hot it is out here? We will drink five or six before it gets dark. I'd say it is probably more like ten, but let's round up to twelve, just to be safe. Remember, these aren't pints we're talking about. They are just little tin cans of beer."

I liked the way he thought. In fact, I had always held the British in high esteem as far as beer drinkers go. "OK, say (2 nights) X (9 people) X (12 beers). How much is that?

"I don't know, mate. I was never good at maths. Shitloads."

I was trying to find a piece of paper and a pen when a girl sitting across from us piped in, "Two hundred and sixteen. It is two hundred and sixteen beers. There is no way you guys are going to need that much beer." I looked around. We had the attention of everyone on the minibus.

"Buy whatever you want for your group, but don't come trying to bum a beer off us when you're dry," Graeme retorted, undeterred by the stares. "OK, we should probably get some wine as well." The girl almost passed out. "I figure one box of red and one of white."

"Sounds good." I smiled. I could tell I was going to like Graeme. When we got to the store, we headed to the booze isle. We diligently compared prices for each brand, and then settled on a fine selection of three cheap local labels. Then we moved on to the wine and performed an equally thorough investigative selection process. We had been in the store about twenty minutes and hadn't selected any food when a voice came over the loud speaker: "Good evening, customers. Can I have your attention please? This store is now closed. Please bring your final selections to the counter for check out."

We stared at each other in complete shock. We were supposed to leave for the island the following morning at 6:00 AM. This was our only chance to buy food. Graeme pushed me a cart, "Go! Go! Go! Head that way. Grab as much as you can. I will go this way! I will meet you at the check-out counter. Go!"

The next few minutes were a blur. I breezed by the store manager who protested, in Doppler effect, "Hey! Stop! Please! SIR! WE'RE CLOSED! You must leave!" I grabbed anything I could get my hands on while racing from the shelf-stockers, who were now in hot pursuit. I was twenty feet from the meat section when I saw Graeme, who was being chased by a couple of janitors.

"Jeremy, we need chicken for the BBQ. I'll block for you. Go! Go! Go!" he yelled. Graeme fought courageously to slow them down as I piled drumsticks, thighs, and breasts into my cart. "THAT IS ENOUGH!" demanded the store manager. "You two will need to leave NOW!"

We were escorted to the cash registers by the store employees, who were heavily armed with mops and price-tag sticker guns. The girl from the van watched us in complete disbelief. As the clerk bagged our rations, we took stock:

- 15 pounds of chicken
- 20 loafs of bread
- 5 bags of chips
- 1 gallon of BBQ sauce
- 1 bag of rice
- 73 packets of sandwich meat
- 2 quarts of butter
- 1 bottle of mayonnaise
- 2 boxes of cereal
- 1 bag of cookies (which Graeme was now eating)
- Enough beer and wine to last a month

We were quite pleased with ourselves. We loaded up our groceries and then headed back to find the others, expecting a hero's welcome. Martin waved as we entered the pub. Graeme flipped him off and then smiled. We sat down and recounted our last hour, smugly awaiting medals for our bravery. Dorothy was first. "You didn't get any non-alcoholic drinks? What about milk for the cereal? And there is no way we will drink all that beer."

Then it was Ann-Marie. "What about fruits and vegetables, Graeme? You didn't get any vegetables?"

Then Sheila. "I hope you got some dish soap. We will need it to wash the dishes."

Boel was next. "Did we get anything for meals besides chicken and rice? Are we going to eat that twice?"

Graeme lost his cool. "Oh, for fuck's sake people. We were being chased by the grocery Gestapo. We didn't have time to think of all these things."

Neil stepped in and saved the day. "If we manage to get through all of that beer, we won't remember what we ate. I think you two did a hell of a job!"

Melvyn backed him up. "Yeah, fantastic job. Plus we can marinate the chicken in the wine if we are looking for variety."

Martin ended the conversation. "To hell with that. I plan to drink all the wine once the beer is gone." The group fell apart with laughter. Graeme and I smiled, feeling slightly vindicated. We all drank well into the evening, winding each other up, solving the world's problems, and discussing the next day's adventure.

The next morning, we boarded a van and headed over to the 4X4 rental company. There we received a briefing about the insurance coverage on our vehicle. It was obvious this rental guy had seen it all. "OK, people, this is a camping trip, not a demolition derby. I can think of no reason why you should need to intentionally ram your mate who is driving another truck. In addition, I can think of no acceptable excuse for why you would ever need to drive the vehicle into the Pacific Ocean. Additionally, the vehicles are not to be driven at night unless there is an emergency. Running out of beer, cigarettes, firewood, or late-night snacks does not constitute an emergency. Your insurance covers normal wear and tear. It is not normal that an engine explodes or that a clutch is left mangled on the beach." He could have been a stand-up comedian, as people were fighting back tears of laughter, but he obviously didn't find it amusing. Years of hooligans trashing his trucks had taken its toll. We were all forced to sign a disclaimer stating that we understood the full financial and emotional rage that would ensue if the truck were damaged. Then we piled in and away we went.

The minute we hit the island, it became evident we had all underestimated the road conditions. Neil was driving, and he was struggling. The truck was violently bouncing over dips and bumps and swerving wildly through the deep sand. We only had a vague idea of where we were going (as no one paid attention during the briefing), and it wasn't twenty minutes until we were lost. Faced with a fork in the road, we all studied our maps and almost evenly came to a split decision. Four lefts. Five rights. So we headed right.

Apparently, the four lefts were better map-readers. The road we had chosen was in a desperate condition, and even worse, it was at a slight ascent. In five minutes we were stuck. This was a very tense moment. A tow would cost $250, not to mention the shame of not even making it thirty minutes into the trip. All of the sudden, everyone was an off-road expert.

"Give it a lot of gas, Neil. Then pop the clutch."

"Put it in reverse, Neil, and then quickly shift into first."

Beads of sweat rolled down his brow. He looked like a panic-stricken madman as he frantically manhandled the gearshift. The cabin of the truck was like a boiler room. Pressure was mounting. Temperature rising.

"Double pump the clutch, Neil."

"Let some of the air out of the tires, Neil."

He was near his breaking point.

"Give it more gas, Neil.

"Not too much gas, Neil. You need to watch your revs."

"SHUT UP. I CAN'T THINK. NO ONE HERE KNOWS SHIT ABOUT OFF-ROADING. SO NO MORE ADVICE. NOW, EVERYONE, GET OUT!!!"

We all stared at each other and then quietly exited the truck. From a safe distance, Martin asked, "So Neil, what are we going to do?"

"I am going to smoke a cigarette to calm my nerves, and then we will try again." I was about to point out that while I didn't know much about off-roading, I was pretty sure a smoke wasn't going to get us out of the rut, but then he added, "And all of you guys are going to push."

Made sense. And it worked. We reversed down the path until we reached the original fork in the road. This time we headed left. Posted markers indicated we were heading toward one of the main lakes, but this road was as grueling as the last. Every few minutes, we'd hammer over a bone-jarring portion of track that left my brain rattled and tailbone bruised.

Finally, we slammed through a huge trough—no, it was more like a gully...no, a ravine...no, a canyon. That's it, a canyon. Everyone went airborne, including Neil. When we landed, somewhere in western Australia, I believe, I saw smoke coming from the back of the truck.

"FIRE!" I yelled. Everyone evacuated. The smoke was coming from underneath our backpacks. Neil and Melvyn bravely tossed aside the bags looking for the source of the smoke. (It was their credit cards that had been left as a deposit for the truck.) Finally, they found it.

"It's our propane tank for the stove. Somehow the regulator was twisted open," Melvyn announced as he shut off the valve. We all stood in astonished disbelief as we waited for the cloud of gas to disperse.

It was Martin who broke the silence, "Well, that is a relief. At least we didn't damage the truck." He reached in his pocket and took out a cigarette.

"NO!!!" Melvyn, Neil, and I shouted in unison.

"What? No time for a cigarette break?" Martin shrugged. Then it hit him. He smiled sheepishly and ducked back into the truck.

Melvyn offered to drive. Neil piled in the back seat with me, and we were off again. Now, there were two things that were particularly bad about the back seat. First, it was an incredibly brutal ride—even more so than the other seats in the truck. You were right over the axel and got to feel every gruesome inch of the road. Second, you were sitting right next to all the backpacks and camping equipment, which would occasionally bounce free and land on your head, fingers, or toes. Every time the truck hit a bump, you would first brace yourself for the landing and then try to protect yourself against the impending attack from a flying flashlight, pair of binoculars, or pocketknife. Just what Neil needed to calm his nerves. Five minutes into Melvyn's driving, one of the coolers landed on Neil's big toe, which was unprotected, as he was wearing sandals. "Aaaaahhhhh," he yelped in pain.

Melvyn stopped the truck, "What's wrong?"

"The cooler landed on my toe."

"But the propane isn't leaking, right?"

"No. It's just my toe. It might be bro—" Before he could finish his sentence Melvyn was off again, like a passionate general pushing his battalion onward to victory. In the trenches of off-road warfare, a broken toe is a mere flesh wound to be tended to once all the dust settles. As the battle progressed, Neil stared ruefully at his toe, and I did my best to ward off other aerial assaults. Then, disaster struck again. "Something is leaking. There is liquid pouring all over the place back here."

The girls tended to the wounded while the men tossed bags aside, looking for the source. It was our twenty-gallon drinking-water bottle. It was about half empty by the time we salvaged it. Our spirits were broken. Our resolve weak. Our determination to push forward wavered.

Then, Ann-Marie stepped up to rally the troops. "OK, guys, there is some good news. Neil's toe is not broken; it is just sprained and bruised." Neil looked unconvinced, but smiled anyway. She continued, "Look, bad things always happen in sets of three. First we got stuck, then we almost blew ourselves up, and now we have soaked all of our clothes, leaving us low on drinking water. That is three. That means the rest of the weekend will be great. Plus, not having much water isn't that big of a problem? We have plenty of beer, right?" She gave Graeme and me a wink.

Everyone smiled. We piled back in the van and were at the lake in no time. Despite our difficult first hour, our group became very close. In fact, it was the initial hardship that brought us together. That evening, we camped on the beach and drank beers around a campfire. In a sign of team unity, everyone was now wearing their blue tour-agent shirts, tailored in a similar sleeveless, V-neck fashion as mine. At some point in the evening, Sheila announced, "We need a group name."

"What about the Smurfs?" Boel suggested. "In honor of our blue T-shirts."

"The Smurfs?" Neil scoffed. "It doesn't sound very tough."

"What about the Mighty Smurfs?" Martin offered.

We fell apart with laughter. Dorothy stood up, "Here's to the Mighty Smurfs!"

"Cheers!" we all shouted, ramming our beer cans into one another's. We were strangers from the four corners of the earth, sitting beneath a majestic fire-orange moon, with waves crashing in the background, enjoying our joint quest of tropical paradise.

Most travelers will tell you that it is not the places you go, but rather the people you meet that make the trip. They are right.

Americans and the British

✦

January 19, 2003
Cairns, Australia

"Giant American corporations are taking over the world. You should be ashamed. It is impossible to travel anywhere these days without seeing the revolting neon glow pouring from the signs of obnoxious American chain restaurants. The entire world is being poisoned by your American culture."

"You should talk. I can't get off a bus without being assaulted by the noise of Robbie Williams, one of the former Spice Girls, or the latest Ministry of Sound CD blaring out of some pub packed with eighteen-year-old British backpackers who are partying their way around the globe, thanks to Mom and Dad's Visa. Plus, if I remember my time in England correctly, American chain restaurants are a drastic culinary improvement for you guys."

"Mate, if it wasn't for that very sense of British adventurism and exploration displayed by the forefathers of those backpackers, your nation wouldn't exist today. As for the food, we tend to focus more on the drink. And speaking of drink, why do you Americans drink all that light beer? I mean, that stuff tastes like piss and has the same alcohol content as apple juice."

"At least we serve it cold. Which brings up the topic of ice. When I left, you guys still hadn't quite mastered the technology required to freeze water in large quantities. Any breakthroughs on that front?"

And so went the ribbing between James and me. It was all good natured though, evidenced by our continual purchase of drinks for each other. Dorothy and I met James and Alice at a hostel in Noosa Heads, a pleasant little beach town north of Surfer's Paradise. They were from Stratford-upon-Avon, the birthplace and home of William Shakespeare, who, James informed me at one point in the evening, "is a famous English poet, in case you Americans haven't heard of him. Maybe you have seen some of his movies?"

They were truly a lovely couple. Dorothy and I had met several people while traveling, but have always particularly enjoyed the companionship of other couples. As luck would have it, James and Alice happened to be in Cairns at the same time we were. It was their final week of vacation, so they had rented a luxurious apartment. When they checked in, they were upgraded to a two-bedroom and graciously offered their second room to us.

In case you can't tell, James and I were somewhat competitive. We challenged each other constantly for three days. We played tennis (he won), chess (I won), swimming (he won), poker (I won), and debated regularly (the winner probably depended on your national loyalties). We even invented new games. Our favorite was ultimate water Frisbee (a distant kin to water polo, I believe). Dorothy and I would represent Team USA and he and Alice, Team UK. On final count, the Americans were up 5-2.

But the funniest game we played was Scrabble. It is worth a quick recount, as it perfectly speaks to the two cultures. See, the British are competitive, but to them, it is more important to show good form and win with honor. Sportsmanship, chivalry, and all that nonsense are the backbone of their competitive spirit. Americans play to win. Period, end of story. I mean, we are the nation that gave the world professional wrestling. ("Oh no. The referee has turned his back, and Mad Dog's going for the chair!") In England, the most popular sport is soccer (football, as they like to call it). In soccer, if a person is injured and the opposing team has the ball, the player will kick it out of bounds to stop the clock and allow the hurt player to receive medical attention. In turn, they lose possession of the ball for kicking it out of bounds. In a sportsmanlike manner, the team of the injured player then voluntarily returns the ball to the other team once play resumes. Can you imagine such a thing in a popular American sport? Of course not. For starters, we would attempt to take advantage of the uneven mismatch presented by one less player on the opposing side. It would be like a power play in ice hockey. Alternatively, if the other team was soft enough to kick the ball out of bounds, there is no way in hell we would give it back to them.

But back to Scrabble. Dorothy was first. I can't remember her word, but it was a respectable twenty-point effort. Then James went. He spelled 'knave,' playing off one of Dorothy's letters. "That means 'an unprincipled, crafty fellow.' Someone like yourself, Texan."

"I am familiar with the word, James. In fact, I used it just the other day while enjoying a spot of tea with a bunch of old ladies," I retorted.

Alice gave me a sneer. "It is a brilliant word, James. Good effort. Now let's see, that is twelve points. Well done."

Next, it was her turn. "I am just so excited you didn't mess up my word." She played vertically off Dorothy's word and laid down 'queen,' apparently the pinnacle achievement among British Scrabble players. She and James were like giddy school children for several minutes. "Oh, me," she sighed, obviously still pleased with herself, "let's see, that is fourteen."

Then it was my turn. I played horizontally off James' 'a' in 'knave' to spell 'farts.' It also worked out that the 's' landed right at the end of Alice's word to form 'queens.'

Alice was flabbergasted. "You can't use the word 'farts!'"

"Sure I can," I answered smugly. "It means to 'to break wind.' An example sentence would be: *When the knave farts, it upsets the queen.*"

Alice turned crimson red and gave a nervous giggle.[1] James let out a hearty English chuckle. "Well played, Texan. Well played."

I smiled. "And including my triple letter score on the 'f,' double word score for 'farts,' and points for 'queens,' that is a score of 47. That puts this knave in a commanding lead."

And I never lost it. I will concede the British have a better grasp of their mother tongue, but in Scrabble, their politeness hinders their chances of victory. This is especially true when paired off against an American who is prepared to stoop to such vulgarities as 'farts' to ensure a win. ('Zit,' 'puke,' and 'crap' were some of my later triumphs.)

---

1.   In England, I believe using the word 'farts' and 'queen' in the same sentence can result in your being banished from the Kingdom.

As with Scrabble, so it is in soccer. I would keep an eye on Team USA in the next World Cup. Mark my words.

Flies, Crocs, and Lizards, Oh My!

✦

January 28, 2003
Kakadu National Park, Australia

Kakadu National Park is located in the north central Australian Outback. If you like flies, this is the place for you. Big flies, small flies, black flies, green flies, annoying flies, biting flies—it has them all. I figure there are one trillion flies in Kakadu. This is not a random guess but an educated estimate. Here's my thinking. During every single moment of my long three days in Kakadu, I had about fifty flies hovering around my face, sunbathing on my neck, or attempting their ultimate martyrdom, the kamikaze dive into my mouth. And the flies didn't seem to be singling me out. No, they were indiscriminate in their torment of all visitors to the park. Most people managed to keep their sanity by wearing fly nets over their faces, but I did see a few nervous breakdowns by one or two unprepared wives whose husbands had convinced them that a camping trip in the Outback would be "fun." One lady had a really bad fit. "Harold, get them off me!" she screamed while spinning in circles and slapping at her face. "They're in my hair. Ah! One's in my ear. They're all over. GET THEM OFF!!!" By the time her husband calmed her down,[1] she was foaming at the mouth, her hair was a mess, and her makeup[2] was smeared all over her face. She looked like a rabid poodle turned loose behind the Revlon counter.

But I digress; back to my estimate of one trillion flies. My point is that I think flies weren't specifically concentrated near me, but were instead equally spread throughout the park. So, I think we can safely assume that my fifty flies accurately represent the number of flies in every square meter of Kakadu. If I consider that the national park is 200 kilometers long and 100 kilometers wide, and then pass all these numbers by my college roommate, who was a math major, one trillion flies is the answer I come to. I don't mean to dwell on this, but that is a lot of freakin' flies. To help put that number in perspective, if you were to squash one fly every second with a fly swatter, it would take you just over 31,688 years to get every one of them (an impossible feat, as Aboriginals have been in this area for at least 40,000 years swatting at flies and haven't been able to put a dent in the population).

I don't want to taint your impressions of Kakadu, though. The park has more than just flies. Take the many beautiful rivers and lakes, for example, which are teaming with man-eating crocodiles. Yes, these picturesque little watering holes would be the perfect place to cool down and escape the ninety-five-degree heat, 100% humidity, and swarming pests—if you don't mind the occasional attack from a colossal reptilian monster. And these predators are fearless, too. The larger saltwater crocodiles can get up to almost twenty feet long and have been known to attack fishing boats. Crocs date back to the age when dinosaurs roamed the earth, and after seeing a couple of crocodile feedings, I have my own little theory about how the dinosaurs became extinct. I think the crocodiles ate them all. So no swimming in Kakadu for me, thanks.[3]

Now, I am sure most of us are familiar with one of Australia's latest personalities, Steve Irwin, "The Crocodile Hunter." For those who don't know him, this guy owns the Australia Zoo and has made several TV shows and movies that feature him feeding crocodiles, picking up poisonous snakes, chasing dragon-sized lizards, swimming with alligators, and performing other death-defying animal

---

1. I sold him my fly net for $150
2. Yes, makeup, in the Outback?!!!
3. Actually, there are a few places to swim in the park where you don't have to worry about saltwater crocs. In these little safe havens, you only need to concern yourself with freshwater crocs, which will usually just rip off a limb rather than try to kill you.

encounters while yelling, "Crickey, would you look at the size of those teeth. This one's a real beauty!" Well, I had assumed this guy was just putting on a show. I was wrong. Our tour guide, Ben, was clearly of the same Irwin lineage. At one point, he slammed on the breaks of the 4X4, threw open his door, and raced out into the bush. The group stared at each other in bewilderment for several moments as we pondered his strange behavior and calculated our next move. Then he reemerged from the brush holding an irate reptile. He gave a goofy smile and said, "This is a frill lizard, everyone. She is a little upset right now, but she is really a lovely little animal. OK, settle down. I am not going to hurt you."

A frill lizard looks something like a gremlin. Not the cute little Gizmo. More like the scary evil ones with of the mouthful of fangs. I kid you not. A frill lizard runs upright on two legs, is about two and a half feet tall, and is all teeth and nails. A gremlin. And this particular gremlin didn't seem to be comforted by Ben's words of reassurance. It was trying with all its might to chomp off his finger or scratch out his eyeballs. Preferably both, I imagine. It hissed, snarled, and thrashed in savage defiance. "Ben, how did you find this lizard?" one of the girls in the group asked.

"Well, I saw it run across the road, so I chased it. I lost it at first, so I had to track it a bit."

"I see. Well, it looks very upset, so you might want to put it down."

"OK, but be on your guard—it might charge one of you."

Let's just say we all immediately lost our interest in frill lizards and high-tailed it back to the safety of the jeep. Ben sat there talking to the lizard for a few more minutes before he put it down. A nice guy, but clearly a little crazy. Maybe the flies got to him after a while.

Anyway, the main reason to go to Kakadu is to get a firsthand look at the park's several fine examples of Aboriginal rock-art paintings. These paintings date back tens of thousands of years and have been repainted by generation after generation. Aboriginals have no written language, so their stories are recorded in their art. One painting depicted a man standing beside a fly and a crocodile. He was staring longingly at the sun, a dingo, a tropical tree, and waves. I think it meant the artist wished his ancestors had decided to settle in Fraser Island rather than Kakadu. But that's just my guess. Heck, he may just have been on the look-out for a ferocious frill lizard.

A Hot, Steamy Night

✦

February 10, 2003
Perth, Australia

Last night, a heat wave moved through Perth, Australia, raising the temperature to 42° Celsius. I believe that is about 512° Fahrenheit. To my complete and total dismay, our hostel didn't have air conditioning. Now, I know many of you from other parts of the world won't find this as appalling as I did, but in Texas, air conditioning is as standard as running water. Houston is perhaps the most advanced city in the world on the air-conditioning scale. Air conditioning is standard in all houses. It is not even considered an optional feature when buying a car.[1] All offices have AC. There is a series of air-conditioned tunnels underneath the downtown area connecting all the skyscrapers. Most nice restaurants and bars even spray a fine air-conditioned mist over the outside patios. Yes, it is a gleaming example of a society which has embraced air conditioning so completely that one needn't ever leave their beloved cooled air. It should serve as a model for all cities where the temperature gets up in the sweat zone.

Last night, I stumbled down to the hostel reception desk and asked if we could be upgraded to a room with air conditioning. Do you want to know what that little air-con-lackey told me? "Sir, none of our rooms have air conditioning. But they all have ceiling fans!"

I stared at him dumbly. "A ceiling fan? Well, fantastic. We'll turn it on and gleefully await the polar bears and penguins to come frolic in the powdery snow drifts that will soon blow through our room." The invention of the fan dates back to about, let's see, 7000 BC, when servants would use palm tree branches to fan the Egyptian Pharaohs. Fans might have been OK back then, but as far as I am concerned, they suck by today's standards.

So I stumbled back to our room and lay next to Dorothy. Trust me, that sort of heat doesn't create a romantic atmosphere. We both lay there, stark naked, trying not to move.

"You're touching me, Jeremy. Get back on your side. I don't want you sweating on my side."

"That's really sweet, honey."

"Jeremy, I am not kidding. Your arm is sweating on my pillow. Now move over."

"Do you not find me sexy, baby? Look at the way the sweat glistens on my beer gut in the moonlight."

"Jeremy, I am not kidding. GET BACK ON YOUR SIDE."

The unbridled passion was truly overwhelming. At any rate, I finally drifted off to sleep, occasionally waking from my dreams of a winter wonderland to turn over my sweat-drenched pillow.

---

1.   Unless you own an old piece-of-shit jeep like the one I drove when I graduated college

Pajama-Jammy-Jam

✦

February 28, 2003
Singapore

A friend once described Singapore as Disneyland run by the Gestapo. Everything is really nice, but if you step out of line, you get the beat down. With this in mind, I exited my airplane on the lookout for the fun police, fearful that I was not in a place which would warmly welcome a wise-ass Texan.

Having been here a few days, I can report that it's not that bad. Sure, they break your legs if they catch you chewing gum,[1] but hey, it's an effective approach. I didn't step in gum once the whole time I was here.

I jest, yet I feel obliged to defend Singapore. I can't quite figure out why. Every building is very modern and has air conditioning (very important after the hostel in Perth). The city prides itself on modern efficiency and convenience. It is located in the tropics and features hot, humid weather almost all year round. It has a huge port and serves as the center of Asia's energy industry. Wait, I got it. Singapore reminds me of Houston, my hometown metropolis. Replace all the Texans in cowboy hats with Singaporeans, and you have a perfect fit. Singapore, Houston's sister city in Asia. I can already envision scores of people on the East and West Coasts of the US rushing to their phones to book their trip.

Anyway, few critics will argue that Singapore is world-class when it comes to embracing cutting-edge technology. And so I present you with a quick travel comedy about a trip to the bathroom in the wee-morning hours.

For dinner that evening, I slurped up some delicious Thai noodle soup and polished it off with a large *Tiger* beer. About 4:00 AM, my bladder was feeling the effects. I slipped out from under the covers and bounded through the darkness of our hotel room with the grace of a gazelle. Once I reached the bathroom, I started patting the wall in an attempt to find the light switch. Instead of a switch, I found the mother of all control panels. No kidding, there were at least twenty buttons, fifteen dials, and five switches on this thing. I really had to pee, so I considered my options:

- Try to find the flashlight in my backpack: Not really an option as it would take too long and I was running out of time.

- Try to find the toilet in the dark: Would probably result in me peeing all over our guest towels.

- Start randomly pushing buttons and flipping switches at the risk of initiating a nuclear strike on some peaceful neighboring country: This was really the only choice I had.

Plus, I'll be honest, I was a little intrigued by all the buttons. I reached out in the darkness and pressed one. The loud, excited voice of a radio DJ blared from the bedside speakers screaming something in Chinese, most likely, "Run for cover. Singapore just launched a nuclear warhead at Beijing." I reached out and pressed the same button again. Now I heard the same voice coming from speakers in the bathroom. I flipped a switch. The TV came on, playing an MTV rock video. I

---

1.   Not really. Feel free to smack your gum loudly and blow huge bubbles. Do it right in front of a police officer. Shoot me an email in five years when you get out of prison and let me know how it worked out for you.

turned a dial. Our window shades started to part. I mashed all the buttons at once in a desperate attempt to turn on a light. The track lighting in the bedroom was activated. It shone brightly, then dimmed, shone brightly, then dimmed. It was as if the whole freakin' room was alive. I had created my own funky little techno nightclub, but at least I had some light. I bounded, a little less gracefully than a gazelle this time, toward the commode.

After I finished my business, I turned to go back to the bedroom. Dorothy was pounding on the panel. She looked over at me with fire in her eyes. She yelled something that I couldn't quite make out over noise pumping from the room's entertainment system. By the look on her face, I don't think she was asking me to dance. Oh well, she's never been much of a morning person.

I went over to the master panel and helped her get the room back under control. We then ran and hid under the covers, hoping that the Singapore police wouldn't come banging on our door for disturbing the peace—or for bombing China.

Sweet People, Spicy Food

♦

March 2, 2003
Bangkok, Thailand

My college roommate, Howie, has an older brother who married a Thai woman he met in graduate school. The two had a huge wedding ceremony in Thailand, and Howie flew over to be the best man. During the festivities, Howie met several members of his sister-in-law's extended Thai family, many of whom are about our age. Last week, Howie sent an email to one of his new Thai cousins, Nuch, telling her that Dorothy and I were coming to Thailand and asking if she would show us around. Nuch happily agreed and arranged to pick us up at the airport. She met us at our terminal with her friend, Am. After talking to Am for five minutes, we discovered she worked at the same management consulting firm where Dorothy and I had spent our last five years. Turns out she even worked in the same industry group and actually knew several of our American colleagues.

What are the odds? I mean, doesn't this just make you want to skip around the room in a childlike glee singing "It's a Small World After All?"

OK, I will quit being a cheeseball.

After they picked us up from the airport, Nuch and Am drove us around Bangkok pointing out temples, monuments, and royal palaces. As we passed one of the most exquisite temples I have ever seen, Nuch said, "That is Wat Phra Kaew. You should go there tomorrow and spend two or three hours walking around and taking pictures."

I wanted to write down the name so I could remember it the next day. Now, if you will think back to my pathetic attempts to learn Spanish in Costa Rica, you will recall that I am hopeless with foreign languages. And languages don't get much more foreign than Thai.

"How did you pronounce the name, Nuch?" I asked.

"Wat Phra Kaew," she responded.

I thought she was saying one long word. "Watfaca?" I asked.

"Wat-Phra-Kaew," she said, slowly and deliberately.

"Wafercew," I tried again.

This was getting a little embarrassing. Dorothy was covering her face, ashamed at my butchery of the Thai language.

Nuch rescued me. "Jeremy, you can just call it the Emerald Buddha Temple. That is what all the Westerners call it. Any taxi driver will know what you are talking about."

"Thanks," I replied.

"Don't worry about it. Most foreigners struggle with the Thai language. It is very common that we make up other words that are easier for them to say. 'Bangkok' is another example. In the Thai language, this city is not called 'Bangkok.'"

"Really? I didn't know that. What is the city's name in Thai?" This one I was going to get right. I thought it would show huge cultural consideration on my part to refer to Bangkok using its proper Thai name.

"Krungthrep mahanakhon amon ratanakosin mahintara ayuthaya mahadilok popnopparat ratchathani burirom udomratchaniwet mahasathan amonpiman avatansathit sakkathattiya witsanukamprasit." Nuch smiled.

"You're joking."

"No, it's the truth," she laughed.

I wasn't even going to try. It would take me three and a half years to learn to pronounce the name correctly, and then it would make for quite long-winded conversation. "Hello, yes I would like to buy a round trip ticket between Hong

Kong and Krungthrep mahanakhon amon ratanakosin mahintara ayuthaya mahadilok popnopparat ratchathani burirom udomratchaniwet mahasathan amonpiman avatansathit sakkathattiya witsanukamprasit please."

"Sorry, Nuch. I am going to have to stick with Bangkok."

"Good choice, Jeremy."

That evening, we had a reservation at an equally hard-to-pronounce new restaurant located on the bank of the Chao Phraya River. Our table was right on the water, and we had a wonderful view of the majestically-lit Saphan Phra Ram IX, the longest single-span cable-suspension bridge in the world. When our food arrived, we were treated to the pleasant smells of coconut, lime, basil, and chilies.

"Be careful of this sauce," Am warned. "It is very spicy."

"Spicy? Ha! I grew up in Texas and was raised on Mexican food. That means *picante, pico de gallo*, and jalapeno peppers. I can handle spicy food." And with that proclamation, I boldly scooped a full spoon of the hot sauce onto my rice.

Tong, another of Nuch's friends who had joined us for dinner, looked worried. "Jeremy, that stuff is really hot. I wouldn't eat it. Let's order you some more rice."

"Tong, my good man, have you ever eaten a jalapeno pepper?" He allowed that he had not. "It is the mack-daddy of all spicy food. I chew on the things like they are candy. Trust me, bud, this hot sauce will pale in comparison to some of the salsas I have tried in various Mexican border towns." And with that, I scooped the rice into my mouth.

I reckon a hand grenade exploding in my mouth would have been more painful, but just slightly. I yelped like a coyote who'd just stepped on one of those steel-jawed traps. Tears flowed freely from the corners of my eyes down the sides of my face. I felt my nose hairs singe, and then completely incinerate. I lost my ability to focus and see colors and could only make out shadow-like figures in various smoky shades. The noise reaching my ears sounded like echoes. "Jeremy-Jeremy-Jeremy are-are you-you OK-K-K-K?" I was coughing so violently that I thought I was going to hurl. I was sweating like a backpacker caught in a heat wave in Perth staying in a hostel with no air conditioning. My tongue felt like it I had spent the last hour or two licking a cheese grater. My spit tasted like volcanic lava, making it sa-lava (I can laugh about this now). I grabbed the large beer sitting on the table in front of me and drained it. I splashed some ice water on my face, then poured the whole glass on my head. Nothing would numb the pain. Between my coughing fits, I was making little gurgling noises. I could feel the spice shredding my insides, first my esophagus, then my stomach, and then my intestines. It was moving through my digestive track at a speed which suggested it would be making an exit in a matter of moments. I shouted at Tong, "Which-which-which way-way-way to the toilet-toilet-toilet???"

I couldn't see him well enough to determine which direction he was pointing. I considered diving in the river, which was right beside us. Drowning would be relatively painless compared to this agony. I spasmodically sprinted towards the front of the restaurant, trying to find the toilets. I got lucky. Fifteen minutes later, after battling with some fierce inner demons, I rejoined the others at the table. I believe I was twenty pounds lighter.

Everyone was very nice and most concerned. Nuch, Am, and Tong all asked if I was OK. The waiter came over, filled my water, and asked if there was anything he could get me. The manager checked to make sure the food was not too hot. I assured them all that I was fine, and that the food was wonderful. I finished dinner, steering clear of the fire sauce.

As we asked for the bill, I noted to myself that Thai people, at least the ones I had met so far, were very friendly. Not just Nuch, Am, and Tong, but the reception staff at our hotel, the employees at the restaurant, and random people we'd come across around town. They were all just so polite, accommodating, and generally happy. I am writing this story several days later, and having now been in Thailand for about a week, I can still vouch that every Thai I've met has had a delightful disposition. Since everyone is so nice, I have to think it has to do with the way they are raised. What parenting technique could prove so effective? I haven't asked, but I have my suspicions that it has to do with the chili sauce. I bet if Little Tong and Little Nuch misbehaved, they knew it was a spoonful of the fire sauce. Heck, that disciplinary technique would have turned me into the most well-mannered young man you can imagine. I might even have turned out as nice as the Thai people.

Anyway, when we were back in Nuch's car, Dorothy leaned over to me and asked, "So, Jeremy, was the sauce hotter than jalapeno peppers?" She giggled, obviously finding herself quite amusing. Apparently there was no spice discipline for her as a child.

"Slightly," I replied.

SCUBA + European Fashion Tips

◆

March 14, 2003
Ao Nang Beach, Thailand

Dorothy met Murdo on her first day of work in London. He was her project manager and immediate supervisor. At first, they made a slightly odd pair. I don't think the formal, well-mannered Scotsman knew what he had signed-up for in agreeing to staff the feisty young New Yorker. The British work culture is assertive, structured, and proactive, but also polite, reserved, and preferably non-confrontational. Polite, reserved, and non-confrontational are not adjectives I would choose to describe most New Yorkers I know. Murdo's status meetings had previously been pleasant, civilized discussions, usually while sipping tea. With Dorothy's arrival, the meetings became a battlefield of verbal crossfire, her fully-automatic tongue packing enough firepower to rattle the cufflinks from his shirtsleeves. Despite this stormy start, the two quickly discovered that while their professional styles differed considerably, they were actually quite similar outside the office, where Murdo's formality disappeared. They soon became good friends and Dorothy received a standing invitation to join Murdo and the team for celebratory end-of-week drinks every Friday at the local pub. After a couple of weeks, Dorothy extended the invitation to me.

The first couple of times I met Murdo, I needed Dorothy to serve as a translator. His thick accent and frequent use of colloquial Scottish expressions sounded foreign to this Texan. I would just stare and nod, smiling when he smiled, laughing when he laughed, and buying the pints when it was my round.

During the next two years in London, Murdo became one of our closest friends. As our wedding approached, we invited him to join us in New York for the celebration. He attended the ceremony in a kilt, the traditional Scottish formal attire. Guys, if you ever want to go to a wedding and impress the ladies, wear a kilt. I am sure it helps if you also have Murdo's Sean Connery good looks and sophisticated accent, but I think the kilt alone would do it. On several occasions, young ladies approached me and said things like, "Hi, you must be Jeremy. I am Samantha. I played basketball with Dorothy back in high school. She has told me so much about you."

"Hello, Samatha. Dorothy and I are so glad you could join—"

"Yes, yes. Anyway, I heard you are friends with the guy in the kilt. What is his name?"

"Ah, right. His name is Murdo."

"MER-do? Is that how you say it?" she asked, glancing over her shoulder at him.

"No. It's mur-DOE."

"OK, thanks." She would then scamper over to him. "Hello MER-do. My name is Samantha. I love your kilt. I just saw *Braveheart* the other day, and it is such a good movie!"

Murdo paused in his dramatic explanation of his family crest to the captivated audience of young ladies and said, "Samantha. Whit a beautiful name. 'Tis a pleasure tae meet ye," and then would gently kiss her hand to the enamored "ahhhh" of his American female admirers. The last time I saw Murdo that evening, he had just informed the ladies that when wearing a kilt, it is Scottish tradition not to wear any underwear (i.e., commando-style). He proudly professed always to honor that tradition. The situation quickly deteriorated to something out of a Chippendales night club, as the woman chanted, "Prove it! Prove it!" waving $20 bills in his face.

Anyway, Murdo was planning to meet us in Thailand for a couple of weeks of SCUBA diving and chilling out on the beach. Dorothy and I had arranged for

Nuch, our new Thai friend, to join us at the airport in Bangkok to meet him. When I saw Murdo clear customs, I gave him a big wave and a smile. We walked over to greet him. "How was your flight?" I asked as Dorothy gave him a hug.

"Aw pal, it wis murder! First, the airline assigned me and this other fellah the same seat, and he ends up getting an upgrade tae first class. The jammie wee sod! So, Ah takes ma seat next tae this wee stoater, who turns oot tae be frae some suburb near Glasgow. But pal, she wouldnae shut up. She wid ask about ma trip and then be like 'Oh, yer goin' SCUBA divin'; that's pure dead brilliant!' an' then talked herself up for the next hour! Whit a ned. Ah jist wanted tae look at this burd and say 'You're nippin' ma heid wumin!' Onyways, the joker oan the other side of me wis obviously oot on the ran-dan last night. He looked like he wis still pissed and he reeked like a lum. Ah thought any moment he wis goin' tae be giving it huey all over me. Aw, but furget a' that Jeremy, we're in Thailand, which means no dreech London weather for two weeks. Now, whiddeyesay tae a wee bevvy? Ah've got sum drouth on me!"

As he spoke, Dorothy translated for Nuch. "Oh pal, it was terrible. First, the airline assigned me and this other guy the same seat and he ends up getting upgraded to first class. That lucky swine. So, I take my seat next to some gorgeous chick, who turns out to be from some suburb near Glasgow. But she wouldn't shut up. She kept asking me about my trip and then would be like, 'You're going SCUBA diving. Oh! My! God! That is like, so cool!' and talk about how great she was. What a ditz. I just wanted to look at this chic and say, 'You're giving me a headache woman!' Oh anyway, the guy on the other side of me obviously went out boozing last night. He looked like he was still drunk and he reeked of cigarette smoke. I thought at any moment he was going to puke all over me. Oh, but forget about that, Jeremy, we're in Thailand, which means no wet, rainy London weather for two weeks. Now, what do you say we get a drink? I am parched!"

As we pulled away from the airport, Nuch graciously insisted that the three of us stay at her family's house that evening rather than pay for a hotel room. We were honored. For dinner, she took us for a great meal in a German brew house that served traditional Thai food. Fantastic!!! After too many steins of beer and more close calls with local spices, we retired to her house for the evening. When we woke up the next morning, Nuch's mother had prepared a traditional Thai breakfast of sweet rice, little dumplings filled with ginger and sugar, fried breads with a dipping sauce that tasted like sweetened condensed milk, pork satay skewers, fresh fruit, and a glass of soya milk. A delicious meal, but probably a bit too adventurous for our still-fragile stomachs, which had been the battlefield in a ferocious fight between the German beer and Thai peppers the night before. Nonetheless, Nuch's family's hospitality was a memorable experience, and as we said our final goodbyes, we made her promise to visit us in New York.

That afternoon, we caught a flight to Krabi, on the coast of the Andaman Sea. From there, we took a taxi to Ao Nang Beach, which was about thirty minutes north. Ao Nang and the surrounding beaches, islands, and rugged cliff coastlines compose the distinctive Thai landscape that is frequently featured on the covers of guidebooks and travel magazines. Unique limestone formations soar from the sea in a grandiose display. Turquoise waves pass over colorful coral reefs to lap against the shores of white sandy beaches. Tropical green vegetation grows along the rock walls. Massive palm and banana trees line the beaches. It is a tropical Eden.

In fact, the only blemish in Ao Nang's beauty is all the European men running around in their Speedos. Now, I have nothing against Speedos, but they have their place. That is, in an Olympic swimming pool on the body of a world-class athlete. A note to all European men who have hijacked tighty-trunks for their own water fashion wardrobe: IT IS NEVER APPROPRIATE TO WEAR A SPEEDO ON THE BEACH! It is especially unacceptable, and arguably criminally indecent, to wear a Speedo if you spent the last fifty years eating too much schnitzel and drinking too much beer. From my previous stories, I hope that you've concluded I have the utmost respect for the gut, and that I myself am quite proud of my own. So this is nothing against guys with big bellies. I am with ya, men! But I will not condone my fellow gutted European brethren running around the beach or lounging poolside in marble-tight trunks. Go buy some shorts, guys. The longer and looser, the better. You will be better men for it and your boys will thank you for their new, unrestricted freedom.

But back to the story. In Ao Nang, we signed up to take our PADI (Professional Association of Dive Instructors) Open Water SCUBA Diving Certification. This course consists of one day of dive theory in the classroom, a second day of practice in the swimming pool, and the final two days on a boat conducting the certification dives. Upon completion of the course, we would have the required credentials to go SCUBA diving with any of the numerous PADI dive operators around the world.

The first day in the classroom was a bit slow, but was entertaining due to the cheesy PADI material. The cover of PADI's *GO Dive* course manual states, "Warning! Contents may lead to high levels of excitement and adventure." Oh boy, I can't wait. The manual opens as follows, "It feels strange the first time. The awkward gear, a bit heavy. You ease into the water and your face slips below the surface. Inhale; the air comes with a reassuring hiss, and for the first time, you breathe underwater…With that first underwater breath, the door opens to a different world. Not a world apart, but different nonetheless. Go through that door. Your life will never be the same."

OK, enough! Let's skip the inspirational bullshit and get to the important stuff, like what to do underwater if a Great White tries to bite me in half.[1] The video was next. I forget the actual name of the video, but I would propose *Welcome to PADI Diving: Check Out What Incredible Bodies Our Dive Instructors Have.* The video did have its redeeming qualities, though. It was filmed in the States and/or Australia, so none of the male instructors were prancing around in Speedos.

I know. I am beating the whole Speedo thing to death. But, Ao Nang happens to be a popular package holiday destination for German, Swiss, and Swedish tourists. So, the Speedos just won't go away. I am as tired of them as you are, but blame the Europeans, not me.

And this leads us nicely into the second day of our dive course, the three of us and our instructor, Alexandra, were in the pool, ready to practice our various SCUBA diving skills. Well, the dive shop shares a pool with the neighboring hotel. Just as Alexandra was demonstrating how to clear her dive mask underwater, one of the hotel guests plunked into the pool. This guy looked like Santa Claus, except instead of wearing his standard red felt suit, he was in—and I am sure you have guessed it—an itsy bitsy, teeny weenie, little yellow male bikini.[2] Now, we four SCUBA divers were sitting on the bottom of the pool in a circle. Alexandra, who was in the 12:00 position, had her back to Mr. Claus. Dorothy was in the 3:00 spot and Murdo was sitting directly opposite her, in the 9:00 slot. I don't think either of them could clearly see Santa because their dive masks restricted their peripheral vision. That left me sitting in 6:00, trying to focus on Alexandra's demonstration directly in front of me, but hugely distracted by the disgusting, full-frontal view of a belly that shook like a bowl full of jelly hanging over a tight-fitting yellow spandex loin cloth. After Alexandra completed her demonstration, we were supposed to take turns clearing our own masks. The idea was to fill the mask about halfway with water, then tilt the head backward and

---

1.   This is actually covered in chapter three. PADI's advice is to "calmly swim along the bottom, keeping an eye on it (the shark)." That night I went and bought a large dive knife and underwater spear gun. Other divers could opt to just keep an eye on the attacking shark as it ate them. I would personally prefer to let that bastard feel the full wrath of modern-day, underwater combat weaponry.

2.   All that were missing were the polka dots.

exhale through the nose. This technique would force air into the mask, effectively clearing all the water. When it was my turn, I filled my mask halfway with water while trying to ignore the visually intrusive gut and banana pouch, but right as I tilted my head back to exhale through my nose, Mr. Claus reached down into his bikini and adjusted himself. I immediately broke into an underwater hysterical laughing fit. During my laughter, I forgot the task at hand and reflexively tried to breathe in through my nose. I realized my mistake as my lungs filled with water. I tried to inhale through the regulator in my mouth, but I was still laughing uncontrollably. I stood up, exploding through the surface for air. The other three immediately rocketed above water as well to make sure I was OK. Poor Santa almost had a heart attack. He must have realized we were there, but I don't think it quite registered that he was reaching down into his Speedo at eye level of a group of people wearing SCUBA masks. It registered now, and he looked mortified. The others were very concerned and kept asking if I was OK. Claus quickly grabbed for a towel and made his exit. I spent the rest of the day trying to block the image from my mind as we continued our underwater lessons.

The third day we finally got out on the dive boat. This was the fun part the three of us had been waiting for. We were on the boat with about twenty other people, most of them German. Every single German on our dive boat smoked. Now, Europe hasn't quite embraced the whole anti-smoking crusade which is raging through the States. There is almost no public place left where people can smoke in the US, and Americans are quite militant about their non-smoking policies. If you are in a sports stadium and someone lights up a cigarette, it's not "Excuse me sir. This is a non-smoking area. Could you please extinguish your cigarette?" No, it is more like, "LOOK! A Smoker! Let's kick the shit out of 'im!" And the angry mob moves in to tear the guy's limbs off. I figure that in about ten years, the US government is going to round up all the remaining smokers and put them in airtight cages in smoking zoos. The nonsmoking masses will then be able to tour the smoking exhibits, while still enjoying their smoke-free environment, and show the dangers of the freakish smoking creatures to their children. "Look in that cage, son. That cage there contains Marlborough Red smokers. They're the most dangerous smokers of all."

"Cool, Dad. Can I have my picture taken with one?"

"No, Billy! Stay back from the glass! The smoke may seep through and get you."

Anyway, if our new dive friends are any indication, I don't think German smokers have anything to worry about for a while. On the way out to the reefs, Dorothy, Murdo, and I sat and mingled with the group. It quickly came up that

I was from Texas. It never fails that when any European finds out I am a Texan, they immediately want to discuss my views on gun control. Most still have a view that Texas is the Wild West, where cowboys and outlaws ride horses and settle their disputes with their pistols.[3] Additionally, many of them have never met a real-life Texan. This is because most Texans would much prefer to vacation within their state.[4] If Texans do decide to leave their state for somewhere foreign and exotic, they usually opt for Louisiana or Colorado. A few of my extremely adventurous statesmen will even venture down into Mexico, but it is uncommon to find them on the streets of Berlin, Paris, London, Rome, or Madrid. Therefore, when a European is presented with the extraordinary opportunity to validate their images of the gun-slinging frontier, it often proves too enticing to pass up. And having found myself in this situation several times before, I am always delighted to oblige.

They wasted no time. "So, what do you think about gun control."

Stock response, "Obviously, there has to be some gun control, or there would be complete lawlessness. I think people should only be allowed to own a gun which is small enough for them to personally carry and fire without the use of a tripod. Once the government starts allowing guys to roll around in trucks with heavy artillery mounted in the back, they are just asking for problems. Although, if the authorities impose a law about mounting weapons on vehicles, then the dove and rabbit hunters will start complaining that their rights are being infringed upon. It is really a complicated issue." This usually stirs excitement.

"Vow! Do you own a gun?"

"Of course."

"How many?"

"Twenty-four, but I only carry three on me at once."

"Vhen do you carry a gun? All the time?"

"No, not all the time. I mean, I wouldn't take one to church or to the doctor's office, but if I am going someplace more dangerous, like say the mall or a school, then I will make sure to have at least a couple of guns with me."

"You are joking!"

"Of course I am joking. I would never go to the doctor's office without a gun! Ha ha!"

"Do you think it is safe for people to carry guns?"

---

3.   I reckon this is because much of Texas is still like the Wild West, where cowboys and outlaws ride horses and settle their disputes with their pistols

4.   Which is understandable. It is the best place on earth.

"Sure. We have to learn how to use them in school, so we know what we are doing." And this goes on as long as I can keep a straight face and tolerate the billowing clouds of smoke.

When the boat finally stopped, we put on our gear and jumped in the water. Diving was incredible. It easily surpassed sunbathing as my favorite sport. When diving, you adjust your weights and floatation devices to achieve neutral buoyancy. The idea is to just float there in complete weightlessness. You glide over an underwater world of brilliant colors and silently observe the foreign and fascinating array of aquatic life. It was so peaceful and relaxing that after our first dive, I felt a bit guilty about making fun of the opening passage of the PADI dive book, however, not bad enough to exclude it from my story. The next day we completed the dive course with two final dives and were hooked for life.

I will conclude with a quick recap of what we have learned:

- Men, it is OK to wear dresses to weddings, but not Speedos to the beach.

- Everyone, be cautious of your actions in the hotel pool. You don't know who is watching and from what vantage point.

- American smokers, defect to Germany and invent a SCUBA smoking apparatus. You will live out your days as a national hero rather than locked in a zoo.

- Finally, learn to dive. It rocks.

Castaway

◆

March 14, 2003
Phuket, Thailand

Our final dive in the PADI certification course was in the protective cove of Maya Bay on the island of Ko Phi-Phi Leh, the much-acclaimed and controversial filming location of Twentieth Century Fox's *The Beach*, starring a young Leonardo DiCaprio. The film was based on the Alex Garland's novel about a group of backpackers' failed attempt to sustain a secretive, self-sufficient beach paradise in Thailand's Ang Thong National Marine Park. The movie's production was protested by environmental activists, who claimed the shoot would wreck the pristine beach, leaving it trashed and trampled. Well, friends, from my vantage point on the dive boat, I am happy to report the following:

1. Director Danny Boyle and crew seem to have left their set in good condition, because this is the prettiest beach I have ever seen.

2. The current group of backpackers on *The Beach* appear to be getting along much better than Garland's characters.

3. I look every bit as sexy as teenage heartthrob Leonardo looked when he was here…well almost.

After we completed our final dive, we boarded a long-tail boat[1] heading to Ko Phi-Phi Don, a neighboring island in the Phi-Phi archipelago. That evening, we enjoyed an incredible sunset and then hit the sack, tired from our two days of diving. The next morning, Dorothy, Murdo, and I caught a ferry to Phuket, the island tourist Mecca of Thailand's Andaman Coast. Many budget travelers and backpackers dismiss Phuket as an overcrowded, overpriced example of everything that can go wrong when the tourism industry moves in and takes over a once-tranquil and remote beach. I would tend to agree with them, unless you can spare 100,000 Marriott hotel points and visit the J. W. Marriott Hotel Resort and Spa. Located on an endless sprawl of white, sandy beach in the remote northern end of Phuket Island, this hotel is a world away from the bustle and noise of the south-western beaches of Patong, Karon, and Kata.

When we checked in, a lady in a traditional Thai robe offered us a green tropical cocktail. Dorothy turned and asked the receptionist what we were drinking.

"A mojito. The James Bond drink from *Die Another Day*."

How cool. "Yeah Baby!!! Yeah!" I said in my best British spy voice.

"That's Austin Powers, ye big jessie." Murdo corrected.

"Jeremy, this is a nice place. Straighten up!" Dorothy reprimanded, giving me a little pinch on the butt.

"Oh, behave!" I continued. Murdo laughed.

"Jeremy, stop it!" Dorothy threatened.

As we waited for our keys, Dorothy wondered aloud, "How much would this place cost if we didn't have our hotel points?"

---

1. These narrow wooden boats are the standard island transport in Thailand. A Thai captain navigates the boat from the rear by controlling a long pole with the propeller attached to the end.

I couldn't resist. I placed my pinky up near my mouth, "One million dollars. Wa-ha-ha."

"Jeremy! Shut up!" She said, digging into my forearm with her fingernails.

This was by far the nicest hotel I had ever seen, and if you can stay for free on points accumulated during endless corporate travel, I would also argue that it is an incredible value. The grounds were a vast spread of infinity pools, waterfalls, and manicured lawns lit by thousands of torches set ablaze at sunset. The beach is so remote that we often had the sand entirely to ourselves. One afternoon, Murdo went on a three-hour walk, and the only other people he encountered were Thai workers who assumed he was lost and offered to share their water.

But what topped it all was the hotel's service. When lounging by the pool, as soon as I would think to myself, "Man, it's hot out here," a pool attendant would be at my side with a friendly Thai smile offering a cold towel lightly scented with lemon and jasmine. After cooling my neck and face with the towel, I would be just about to think, "I am getting a little hungry," when another smiling employee would offer me pieces of complimentary pineapple. Truly remarkable.

However, the most extraordinary of these little niceties was the fresh flowers placed on my pillow. It wasn't just the flowers themselves that made the experience so rewarding, but rather the fact that anytime I left the hotel room, I would return to a new flower replacing the previous one. It took me a couple of days to pick up on this, but from then on, I was captivated. I would slip out on our patio to enjoy the ocean view, and when I returned to the bedroom, a NEW FLOWER. It became a game. I would hide behind the curtains, straining to hear the door open and the soft pitter patter of bare feet moving across the tile. I could never hear anything, but every time I re-emerged, a NEW FLOWER. It's like little Thai flower ninjas were moving in stealth through my room and disappearing without a trace.

The hotel also offered all sorts of water-sports equipment for the enjoyment of their guests, free of charge. Given my propensity for making a fool of myself, I decided to see if I was any better at windsurfing than I was at catching waves on a long board in Costa Rica. Having now tried them both, I can conclude that I am comically inept at all aquatic sports that require balance.

I tried windsurfing a few years ago, but I decided it would probably be a good idea to get a demo from the Thai beach boy employed by the hotel. He explained that the basic idea of windsurfing is to stand on the board and then pull the sail up out of the water with the attached rope. Then, the wind should fill the sail and the speed and direction of the board could be controlled by the angle of the sail. Simple, right?

Balancing on a stationary board was hard enough. Standing up on a board that was moving up and down over incoming ocean swells verged on impossible. After about thirty minutes, I learned to time the pauses in the wave, and finally found my footing.

Once on my feet, I tried to lift the sail. Hoisting a submerged sail is hard work.[2] In order to avoid being toppled forward by the resistance of the sail, I had to lean backwards. This required even finer balance. The slightest change in wind or the smallest unexpected wave sent me right off the board, ripping the rope from my rapidly blistering hands.

But on the tenth attempt, I succeeded! Once standing, I just held onto the sail and went in the direction of the wind. When the board was moving across the water, it is much easier to remain balanced. Wahoo! This was more like it. I cruised through the water like a pro for about five minutes before a gust of wind blew me over.

Now, in the joy of my success, I hadn't paid much attention to the direction of the wind. I looked back toward the shore. I was at least 1000 feet out from the beach and faced a strong offshore breeze. I knew I needed to cut in a crisscross pattern into the wind at roughly a forty-five-degree angle if I wanted to head back to the beach. After several failed attempts, I was completely exhausted. The latest tries ripped the blisters on my palms, and they were now bleeding. I needed another plan.

I thought back to surfing. In Costa Rica, I often paddled great distances on my surfboard in order to reach the outer breakers. So maybe I could just paddle this board back in. Negative. The sail attached to the board right where my crotch need to be. Lying down on by stomach to paddle the board was not an option if I ever wanted to have children.

So what was left? Swimming and pulling the board behind me? At the risk of giving away the plot, one of the setbacks Garland's backpacker beach community suffered was a shark attack. Having read *The Beach* only weeks before, the prospect of swimming back to shore with my hands bleeding wasn't very appealing.[3] I decided to lie on the board on my side to consider other options and gain some strength and courage. I closed my eyes and drifted under the heat of the sun and the meditative motion of the waves.

---

2.   Or perhaps I am just a weenie.
3.   Note to self: dive knife and spear gun should be carried for all aquatic sports, not just SCUBA diving.

A cold splash of water in the face startled me back to full consciousness. I stared at the shore. The wind had blown me out another 200 feet. I could probably still make the swim, but there was no way I could tow the board. Plus, the sun was starting to set—prime shark feeding time. Even if I successfully made the swim, this was a bad situation. What was I going to say? "Ah, sorry but I seem to have lost your windsurfing board."

Then, I felt another splash of water. I looked over to determine its source. The Thai beach boy from the hotel slapped the water with the paddle from his sea kayak, sending another spray my way.

He smiled. "You did very good for first day. Tomorrow, I teach you to turn around."

To my intense relief, he took over the windsurf board, and I settled into the kayak. Still smiling, he pulled up the sail and took off toward the beach, tacking at perfect angles.

Now my pride returned. I was not going to let this kid beat me back to the beach. I started paddling with everything I had, just like I was taught by Master Yoda in Pucon, Chile. With sweat pouring off my brow, I looked over to see how the kid was doing. He was catching air off the waves. What a showoff! The nose of my kayak rammed into the sand just seconds before he arrived at the shore.

As I panted for air and stared woefully at my bleeding palms, he came up and took my kayak and started dragging it up the beach.

"I can help drag it if you want," I offered.

"No. You hotel guest. I pull kayak. You go to pool and have mojito!"

Bless you, son. I stumbled along the beach and headed to our room, opting to skip the pool until I bandaged my wounds. I entered the room and searched through our bags for our travel medical kit. From the corner of my eye, something caught my attention. I looked over toward our bed. On top of my pillow, a NEW FLOWER.

Ninja

◆

April 1, 2003
Tokyo, Japan

Interested in traveling to Japan? I highly recommend watching *The Sopranos*, *Goodfellas*, *The Godfather*, and *Casino*. I know these shows are about Italian-American organized-crime families, they don't cast a single Japanese character, they aren't filmed in Japan, and as far as I remember, they don't even mention Japan in any part of the plot. Furthermore, I am not suggesting that in Japan you can expect to get stabbed by some guy named Mack the Knife because he thinks you are moving in on his turf. Quite the opposite, Japan has one of the lowest crime rates in the world. So why should you watch all these movies about the mob? Because it will help you pack! You with me? No? What does every single character in each of those movies carry with them at all times? No, I'm not recommending you pack heat, although I am proud of you for thinking about your right to bear arms. The answer? Stacks of cash. Not traveler's checks, not personal checks, not credit cards, not ATM/pulse cards, not letters of credit, not government bonds, not certificates of deposits, not any other kind of legal tender. Just cash. And they carry heaps of it. So when you pack for Japan, toss out your tried-and-trusted packing list of key vacation items like Hawaiian shirts, sombreros, Mardi Gras beads, and *US Diplomat* business cards. Leave all that stuff at home and instead pack neatly piled stacks of crisp $100 bills. Take at least $1 million. If you watch the movies I recommended, then you should have no problem fitting all that cash in one large suitcase. If you have any room left, then you can throw in a few Hawaiian shirts.

Most people have heard Japan is expensive, but few know it is still primarily a cash-and-carry society. The majority of stores, restaurants, hotels, and bail bondsmen don't accept credit cards, and hardly any ATM machines recognize international pulse cards. So, I am quite serious about needing to take lots of cash.

In our travels to date, we relied solely on credit cards and cash machines. Our trusted plastic served us well in Costa Rica's rain forests, the Andes Mountain Range in Peru, Chile's deserts, Patagonia's Arctic wilderness, Australia's Outback, and the tropical islands of Thailand. But our cards were of no use to us in Tokyo's Shibuya district, Japan's ultra-modern version of Time Square teaming with yuppie, techno-gizmo enthusiasts using their email-enabled mobile phones with integrated digital camera to take pictures of plasma-screen-billboard advertisements showing the new matchbox-size Sony laptops.

Luckily, we were meeting our friends, James and Rika, who live in Tokyo. James was my best friend in high school, where we played on the tennis team together. He was born to be an attorney. This kid could argue about anything and everything. He lived for verbal sparring. After a high school career of tormenting teachers who dealt him any sort of perceived injustice, James went off to college and then to law school. He met his wife, Rika, who is Japanese, while studying law in Japan. Upon graduating, they both took jobs with large, prestigious Japanese firms.

James, and most other attorneys, will be quick to point out that lawyers do more than just argue. This is true. They also have the daunting responsibility of cashing very large paychecks and trying to spend all that money. So, if you don't have an entire suitcase full of $100 bills when you show up in Japan, at least make sure you have a friend who is a corporate attorney in Tokyo with a nicely padded Japanese checking account.

This strategy is not without its risks, however. James quickly crafted a contract for a short-term loan with a structured repayment schedule against a compounding-variable rate based on a composite index of my consumer credit rating, various federal interest rates, and the Yen/Dollar exchange rate, with an additional clause specifying penalties for early and late payment. Given my weak negotiating position, I signed my life away after only a quick skim.[1] He withdrew enough cash to last us a couple of weeks,[2] and we headed to dinner.

To get to the restaurant, we needed to take the subway. There are approximately 6 billion people in the world. I believe 5.9 billion of them can be found on the Tokyo subway during rush hour. It reminded me of when I was a young boy and would kick the tops off anthills.[3] I was always surprised not only by the number of ants, but how they seemed to move in such coordinated confusion. The Tokyo rush-hour crowd flowed in the same anthill-autopilot mode. Commuters walked with their heads down, mesmerized by their mobile phones, thumbing text-messages with *Matrix*-like speed while staring at the display panel as if it were an air-traffic-control radar screen navigating their flight pattern through the station. Packed trains sped by the platform with Japanese businessmen plastered against the windows like ice hockey players being checked into the glass. The platform was crammed, yet people respectfully formed distinct lines for the trains. The sense of calm order amongst such crowded chaos was bizarre.

I turned to James. "I'm surprised people are courteous enough to form lines to get on the subway. In London and New York, people just mass on the platform and then muscle their way onto the subway when the doors open. The strong make it; the weak wait for the next train. No one would even consider forming a line."

He smiled. "In Tokyo, everyone makes it on the train. No one waits for the next one."

I frowned. The doors of our train opened and Japanese commuters poured out onto the platform. Even after the flow from the subway ended, the car still appeared impossibly full. Then, our line surged through the open doors.

Now, let me take a quick break to address the smug "no big deal" responses from the veteran rush-hour subway commuters out there in other big cities. I spent a couple of years commuting in rush-hour traffic on the tube in London and the subway in New York. I know your mental image of a crowded subway car. Triple that number of people and you will have a picture of the Tokyo subway rush-hour crowds. Still not believers, are you? OK, here's one for you. The

---

1.   My only other option was to try and sell Dorothy. With her blond hair and light eyes, she would have probably fetched a good price, but I thought back to her mother's threats about the shotgun.

2. $250K, which should be plenty for fourteen days if you are a budget traveler.

3.   Because this is how one entertains oneself as a young boy in Texas.

Tokyo subways employ large, gloved men whose sole job is to stand on the platform by the door and push stray body parts into the cars so the doors will be able to close. Sometimes, it takes four or five of these guys pushing with all their might to pack the crowd through the doors. Not smirking now, are you. If some guy with latex gloves started shoving London commuters into the train, the male passengers would slap at him with their umbrellas and *Financial Times* until one of the female commuters punched the guy out. In New York, the gloved assailant would be stabbed repeatedly by schoolchildren, elderly grandmothers, or city-counsel representatives—whoever could get to him first—and then left for dead as rat food.

During my time as a London and New York underground commuter, I remember being close enough to my fellow travelers to notice, "Man, this guy needs some deodorant," or, "This lady needs to lay off the perfume." Here I found myself able to make much more intimate observations like, "This guy needs to clean out his ears," and "This lady could benefit from a scalp moisturizing treatment." These are not the sort of observations I could make about complete strangers without being able to stick my eyeball right in the person's ear canal or right against their scalp. Fortunately, a Tokyo subway ride afforded me such an opportunity, and I can happily tell you that most Japanese are very hygiene conscious. Well, compared to me, anyway. I couldn't tell you what they now think of Texans.

We finally arrived at our stop and crashed out onto the platform like a wave on a beach. I had hardly found my footing before I was caught in a human riptide heading back into the car. James grabbed me by the collar and pulled me out of the current, obviously interested in protecting his investment.

Early that day, Rika called to get us a reservation at Ninja, a popular theme restaurant. As we approached the entrance of the restaurant, the hostess clapped twice, and our ninja waiter jumped out of some hidden panel, landing in a crouched position. "Gaijin no mina, youkoso oidenasatta! Minanomono, kin wo zakuzaku motte maittaka. Aruiwa kanemochi bengoshi kara kinsen-dasuke wo tanomuzo, nazenara warera no yashiki wa tadaja kaeraseneizo."[4]

The ninja escorted us to our table which had *seiza* seating, the traditional Japanese style where guests sit on the floor in front of a low table. At first, I really liked sitting on the floor. However, after thirty seconds, I realized *seiza* is actually

---

4.   Ninja speak for, "Welcome foreigners! I hope you brought a big bag of money or have rich attorney financial backers, because you will not leave this ninja house without spending a fortune."

a modern-day ninja torture device designed to lure Westerners looking for a Zen-like experience and then punish them with back pain and leg cramps. I am about as limber as an ice sculpture. My idea of stretching is reclining in my La-Z-Boy. I still confuse the words Yoga and Yoda. Five minutes into the meal, my spine felt like it was being wrung like a wet towel. I watched other Japanese guests to see how they were coping with the pain. Apparently the trick is to drink about twenty glasses of sake, Japanese rice liquor. While this numbs all pain, it makes it very difficult to use chopsticks. Nevertheless, I would still recommend the sake approach. While it is somewhat embarrassing to have grains of rice dripping from your chin, clinging to your shirt, and matted in your hair, this is by far a better option then suffering through the *seiza* spine torture.

The dinner was extraordinary. Highlights included tuna sashimi[5] served over dry ice (with smoke flowing from the bowl and pouring over the table) and a green tea ice cream with chocolate cake served in the shape of a *bonsai* tree. Unfortunately, the bill was also extraordinary. So if you come to Ninja, make sure you bring the suitcase full of cash that we talked about earlier. Not only will you need it to cover the bill, but it will also make a nice back support while sitting on the floor. If you didn't bring a suitcase of cash on your trip and have no Tokyo-based lawyer friends to help cover the bill, *fuggedaboudit*.

---

5. Thin slices of raw fish—much better than it might sound when complemented with twenty cups of sake.

Mickey Has Nothing on Me

◆

April 4, 2003
Tokyo Disneyland Resort, Japan

After hanging out in Tokyo for a few days, we headed to the Tokyo Disney Resort. We stepped back into our childhood as we entered the gates of the Magic Kingdom and caught our first glimpse of the Disney characters. "It's Mickey," I yelled, "and he's wearing a Kimono!" Japanese kids flew apart like bowling pins as I exploded through the swarms of families. When I put my arm around Mickey, a hush fell over the crowd. I stared into the excited, startled eyes of about 10,000 Japanese children. Rika leaned over and quietly explained, "Japan is still ethnically and culturally homogeneous. There are very few foreigners here. Many children who live outside of central Tokyo have never seen a foreigner before. They will look at you guys like you are celebrities while you are here."

She was right. The kids had completely lost interest in the Disney characters. We were the new hit. The hush was replaced by a new excited buzz. One little boy exclaimed with unbridled excitement, "Mama, ano futotteru gaijin to shashin toritaiyo."

"What did he say, Rika?" I asked.

"He told his mother he wants to have his picture taken with you," she responded.

"How do you know he was talking about me?"

"Because he said he wants his picture taken with 'the chubby foreigner.'"

Atta boy! I posed with him, giving my best grin. He looked so pleased that I thought he was going to ask for an autograph. Then again, he might have. He was speaking to me in animated Japanese, and my Japanese is even worse than my Spanish.[1] After a couple more shots, we made our way through the camera flashes and headed toward the rides.

Space Mountain in Tokyo was almost the same as in the USA. Visitors walked for three hours through a cattle-fenced, space-age labyrinth to finally board a forty-five-second rollercoaster ride into the darkness of a giant planetarium. The only difference worth reporting is that in Japan park guests can obtain a "fast pass," which allows them to return to the ride later in the day and skip the line.[2] So, if a family comes at say, 8:00 AM, they can collect a pass to ride the roller coaster at 4:00 PM without having to wait in line. I have always hated lines, especially ones that move forward at the speed of a charging glacier, but I generally found a little solace in the camaraderie developed with others in the line. A "fast pass" lane eliminates any chance of camaraderie. The first hour of waiting, I watched fast-passers walk by with a sense of envy, yet rational understanding. By the second hour, my view had darkened considerably. By the third hour, I was attempting to incite a violent mob among my fellow line-waiters—to rise up against the fast-passers. "We can no longer be oppressed by these fast-passers and the line-cutting institutions they represent! We must rebel and take control of our own destiny! Here comes a family of fast-passers. Let's get them!"

None of my oppressed brethren quite went along with it.

After Space Mountain, we decided to get lunch. We waited another couple of hours to order our food,[3] and then sat down to enjoy our quarter-size hamburgers and seven fries. As I took my first bite, a young Japanese boy, who was gawking at James and Rika, loudly proclaimed, "Mama, mite. Nihon-jin no onna no hito to Amerika-jin no otoko no hito ga issho ni iruyo!"

---

1.   Much worse.
2.   The Disney parks in the States might have implemented this infuriating practice now, but they didn't have it when I was there.
3.   Thankfully there are no fast passes for the cafeteria.

Rika, who was a bit tickled, leaned forward and whispered the translation, "He said, 'Mom, look! A Japanese girl with an American boy!'"

His mother ignored the comment, hoping her non-response would deter his interest and resolve the embarrassing situation. This kid was intrigued and did not want his mom to miss such a sight, "Mama, miteyo! Sugu tonari ni irujan! Nihon-jin no onna no hito to Amerika-jin no otoko no hito dayo!"

Rika repressed a slight giggle. "He said, 'Mom, look! Right beside you! A Japanese girl with an American boy.'"

The mother was melting into her seat and continued to ignore him. There was no way he was going to let this go. He stood up and pointed at us. "Mama, Sugu soko! Nihon-jin no onna no hito to Amerika-jin no otoko no hito dayo."

Rika, who was still amused but a little embarrassed for the mother, continued to translate, "Mom, look! Right there! A Japanese girl with an American boy!"

By this point, James and I, who each have the subtlety of a malfunctioning bulldozer, cracked up and waved at the boy. The kid seemed thrilled to finally be acknowledged. The horrified mother quickly scooped him up, grabbed their food, and moved to some seats outside.

This gave me a brilliant idea. These Japanese kids didn't want to see animated Disney characters running around in bulky costumes and glued-on smiles. No, they wanted to see foreigners. I plan to write a letter to Disney management suggesting a new Japanese Disney character, White-Guy Willy, played by yours truly. I could just walk around the park entrance in a baseball cap, blue jeans, and a T-shirt. Mickey would be yesterday's news. The Japanese kids would shun that little Asian-caped rodent the minute they saw White-Guy Willy. Heck, I could even work Dorothy into my plans. She could be Gaijin Gretchen.[4] If things went well, I could call up friends in the States and recruit them as well. They could be Black-Man Bradley, Latino Lisa, Native-American Nancy, Polynesian Paul, and Arabian Andy. We would all be stars. Soon we would be the highlight of the Tokyo Disneyland. Disney would give us our own section of the park. Right next to Tomorrowland would be our new Racially-Integrated Island. Featured rides could include the Caucasian coaster and the Hispanic high drop.

While the Japanese youngsters are captivated by the magic of Disney, they are also equally curious about the growing diversity of the twenty-first century. Such is the beauty of the mind of a child.

---

4.   GUY-jean: Japanese for foreigner. When young Japanese children see a foreigner, they will often whisper to each other, "Gaijin! Gaijin!"

Oh yeah, and I would not allow any fast-past lines in Racially-Integrated Island.

Strength of a Samurai

April 9, 2003
Kyoto, Japan

If you want to see Japan at its finest, you can't beat a trip to Kyoto while the cherry blossoms are in bloom. These enchanting trees line many of the main streets and decorate the gardens of most of the city's 2000 temples and shrines. They blossom only once a year, usually for about two weeks in April, signaling the arrival of spring with millions of delicate pink and white petals. Rika, who was determined not to let our view of Japan be largely shaped by an American amusement park, planned a four-day trip to visit her nation's cultural capital, Kyoto.

109

For our accommodations in the city, Rika reserved rooms in a couple of different *ryokans*. There are several defining characteristics of these traditional Japanese inns. The minimalist rooms feature a low table placed on a *tatami* floors.[1] Bedding is a futon mattress, kept folded in the closet during the day and laid on the ground at bedtime. Finally, all guests bathe in single-sex communal baths. The standard bath design consists of a large hot tub surrounded by shin-high showerheads and small sitting stools. The idea is to sit down on the stool and take a shower first and then enjoy a nice soak in the tub.

Yesterday morning, I dressed in my Japanese robe and slippers and headed down for my first *onsen* experience. I've never had any problems with communal showers, as long as everyone minds their own business. I planned to skip the hot tub, as I wasn't thrilled at the prospect of soaking in the nude dude stew, but that part was optional anyway. When I got down to the bath, it turned out I had the place all to myself. So I strolled on in, sat on my stool, grabbed the showerhead, and started rinsing off.[2]

Right about the time I was shampooing my hair, in walks some western guy with his four-year-old daughter following right behind him. Let me send a very clear message to all parents on behalf of men who are not fathers: Intermingled adult-child nudity makes us very uncomfortable, especially if the child is of the opposite sex. I know that some internal switch flips when you become a parent and you are instantly besieged by the strange, yet socially accepted urge to gather all the neighborhood children for a skinny dip in the bathtub while you record the whole thing on home video. But for those of us who don't have kids, it doesn't seem quite so natural. In fact, even writing about this makes me squirm. I just know there is some psychologist out there tracing my feelings back to some traumatic event of yesteryear—perhaps an unfortunate streak down the old slip-n-slide where I blistered my privates on a dry patch or maybe a miscalculated nude belly-flop in the neighbor's kiddy-pool, where I accidentally racked myself. I assure you, none of these are the case. Running around naked in front of little girls makes us non-dad squeamish. It's that simple.

Anyway, I finished my shower and got the hell out of there ASAP. Our first activity for the day was a Japanese costume makeover. The studio planned to turn Dorothy and Rika into *maikos*[3] and James and me into samurais. The girls went

---

1.   Japanese rugs made from finely woven strands of bamboo.
2.   Ladies, control yourselves. I know the image of me sitting nude on a stool with streams of water sensually flowing over my gut is a real turn-on, but this is a PG-13 story.

first. The artist did an incredible job. I couldn't even tell it was Dorothy, but you needn't take my word for it:

Next, it was the boys' turn. When it came time for our pictures, the photographer wanted to pose us individually. James and I had other ideas. Did she really think she could dress two alpha males up as Japanese warriors, arm us each with a deadly sword, and then expect us to pose in wimpy individual profile shots? Hell no. We want live-action fight scenes. It is fair to say that most Japanese are a touch more reserved than most Americans, and it is an absolute certainty that this photographer was more reserved than James and me. She was shocked beyond comprehension as my sword swooshed through the air, missing James' torso by mere inches. When I blocked his counter-attack with a mighty sword clash, she looked as though she might faint. Finally, a truce was reached, allowing us to stage fight scenes so long as we didn't kill each other. The shots were classic. I am sure we will be on the cover of their brochure.

Next, we were off for a hike around one of Kyoto's shrines. At the end of the hike we came up on an *omokaru-ishi*, which translates literally to *heavy or light stone*. We watched a couple of elderly Japanese ladies walk before the stone, which was about the size of a bowling ball and rested on an altar at shoulder level. They bowed their heads, stood for a moment of silent reflection, and then attempted to lift the stone. It didn't budge as their hands trembled with the strain of their exertions. Rika explained, "The idea is that you walk in front of the altar

---

3. Women in training to become geishas, ladies who are part of a Japanese sisterhood trained in the cultural arts to perform for prominent Japanese men.

and make a wish. You then attempt to lift the stone. If the stone is heavier than you expected, it will be difficult for your wish to come true. If it is lighter than you expected, then it will be easy for your wish to come true."

During Rika's explanation, a couple of teenage girls attempted to lift the stone. No luck. I asked Rika if it would be appropriate for me to try. She assured me it was, but emphasized I should remain focused and respectful during the attempt. Dorothy shot me a look that said I had better not screw this up.

As I stepped before the stone, a crowd gathered around, eagerly waiting to see if the Texas gaijin could do the impossible. I stood powerfully, head lowered in meditative preparation. I then slowly lifted my gaze until my eyes were locked on my foe. "YOU WANT A PIECE OF ME, STONE?!!" I screamed in my mind. My eyes blazed, my muscles burned with fury. I stepped forward and grabbed the stone in a steely grip. I bent my knees, tilted my head back, stared at the heavens, took a deep breath, and then exploded into a power lift, just like it was my usual 500 pounds loaded on a squat rack in the weight room.

The stone weighed about as much as a cantaloupe. I heaved it up with such forced that it slipped from my hands. The crowd released a startled gasp. I managed a last-minute recovery, narrowly avoiding shattering the thousand-year-old relic.[4] I was extremely embarrassed. The grandmothers, who had probably staked their grandchildren's education on their wish, glared at me. The two teenage girls, who had probably wished to find true love, shook their heads in disgust. I hung my head and walk back to Rika and Dorothy, who looked very ashamed, and James, who was cracking up.

So, what did I wish for? I wished that I would never again suffer the awkward embarrassment of bathing in the presence a young girl. That night we checked into a new *ryokan*. It was much more modern than the first and had private baths in each room. Maybe the old Japanese wishing stone holds some mysterious powers after all.

---

4.   Editor's note to author—Are you sure about this? The Japanese aren't in the habit of allowing people to touch thousand-year-old relics. In the two years I lived there, every thing I saw of remote archeological value was kept under glass. It was probably a replica.

Author's response to editor—Possibly. I didn't carbon date the freakin' thing. Sigh.

Jet Fuel

✦

April 15, 2003
Somewhere in Russian Airspace

A poem about our flight from Japan to Italy.

"We've been cleared for take off
With no further delay,"
Claimed the frustrated pilot
On the airplane's PA.

"Please bring your seats forward
To their upright angle,"
Sang an attendant named Mary
In a well-rehearsed jangle.

It was a twelve-hour flight
To Rome, where we'd land,
So I thought I would nap,
At least that was the plan.

I was drifting to sleep
When my nose was attacked
By an offensive smell—
A right sulfury smack.

My eyes shot wide open
To see where it started,
Because one thing was clear,
Yo—somebody farted.

Now who would do that?
I mean who could it be?
There was one thing to do:
Look around me and see.

To my left was a Frenchmen.
Was he venting frustrations
About transatlantic rifts
In diplomatic relations?

Or could it be Dorothy,
Looking sweet as could be?
I've smelled her toots before
They're like fresh potpourri.

No, it couldn't be her.
Man, there it was again.
"Can I take your drink order?"
Mary asked with a grin.

Could it be sweet Mary,
With her innocent smile,
Vapor-trailing passengers
As she moved through the aisle?

My friends, I've concluded
That Mary was the source,
Because the smell returned
When she served the food course.

When she walked by, I grabbed her:
"I don't like this one bit!
Every time you come by,
Well, it just smells like…

Sewage or sulfur
Or something quite crass.
I've determined the source
And I think it's your…

Job to make sure that
The air is oxygen rich.
So I hope it'll smell better,
You understand me, you….

Are a hard worker
And that's pretty clear cut,
But your antics upset me
Now get out of here…

Please." OK, I'm lying.
I'm just having a play.
But I thought I would tell you
What I *wanted* to say.

The House of Sonnenburgoni

✦

April 20, 2003
Venice, Italy

Dorothy and I first came to Italy in the summer of 2001 to attend a business conference in Rome. The conference brochure indicated that the presentations
would be in English. We must have missed the small asterisk which clarified that
these would actually be English translations of Italian speeches. If you have never
experienced the excitement and thrill of sitting through three days of monoto-
nously translated speeches delivered via an uncomfortable earpiece, I can assure
you, few other experiences on earth can compare.[1] But hey, I am not complaining. We got to spend the weekend visiting the Roman Forum, the Coliseum, the
Vatican, the Sistine Chapel, the Pantheon, and the Spanish Steps. We had an

---

1.   Except perhaps a dramatic reading from the works of one the great Nebraskan poets
      of the late nineteenth-century, or maybe a pantomime performance depicting the life
      of an amoeba.

amazing time. We loved the city so much that we both agreed it would be the perfect place to start the European leg of our current trip.

When we touched down in Rome last week, my first priority was to find some good Italian food. Pizza. Spaghetti. Garlic bread. Ravioli. Lasagna. Who can argue with Italian food, right? I'll tell you who. The Italians!

I know what you're thinking. "Jeremy, what on earth are you talking about? I might believe some of your crazy tales about places like Patagonia, but I went to Europe for a summer. I know they have plenty of good Italian food in Italy. If you can't find good Italian food nearby, then you're in the wrong country. You're probably sitting in some coffee shop in Amsterdam, dazed and confused. Consult your guide book, buddy."

Don't fret dear reader; I am not in Holland having a schmoke-ana-pancake. I am most definitely in Italy and am of sound mind. I believe you misunderstood me. I never said they don't have good Italian food in Italy. There are quaint side-walk cafés on every street corner, each serving great Italian food. All I said is the Italians don't eat Italian food, at least not until they're over fifty. Younger Italians maintain a strict diet of espressos and cigarettes. Italian food itself is primarily an export product shipped over to America. The only domestic consumers are tourists and retired Italians.

You don't believe me? Go to the nearest retail store for one of the famous Italian fashion houses. Gucci, Prada, Versace—any of them will do. Now, go pick out the biggest shirt you can find. Ladies' or men's, it doesn't matter. Now hold it up and notice how big it is. You remember when you could fit into that, right? Yeah, it was about the time you were learning how to walk. Now that doesn't look like a size made for someone who feasts on pizza and breadsticks with any sort of regularity, right?

Solely espresso and cigarettes, my friends. The next big diet trend in America. You heard it here first. But no fear, when we arrived in Rome, I ate enough pizza and pasta to make up for three generations of skinny Italians. And since I can't fit into any of the Italian designer labels, I am thinking about starting my own Italian fashion line: Sonnenburgoni: ghetto-fly garb for the carb-lovin' mobster.

"Ciao, big boy. Is that a Sonnenburgoni sports coat you're wearing?"

"Ciao, bella. Why, yes it is. Only the finest threads for this carb-lovin' mobster."

So go ahead and eat all the Italian food you want. I will keep you looking ghetto-fly fabulous in the latest wave of Italian fashion.

Yes, the Italians do love their fashion, and not just clothes. They love accessories, as well. Shoes, belts, purses, and most importantly, sunglasses. All Italians wear cool sunglasses. And I mean all Italians. Police officers, street vendors, construction workers, young hip model types, school teachers, gondola guides,[2] waiters, bakers, grandparents, garbage collectors, train conductors, priests, and nuns.

I love sunglasses. They are easily the single most important fashion accessory. It doesn't matter what you are wearing—put on your shades, and you look cool. If you leave the house in ripped jeans and a sweat-stained T-shirt, you look like a bum. Throw on your Ray-bans and you look like a rock star. No other fashion accessory can make such an impact, not even a Sonnenburgoni suit. And there is one other great thing about sunglasses. No matter how much weight you gain, they still fit. After about a week in Italy, my jeans are feeling a little snug, but my sunglasses are still nice and comfy.

Anyway, back to the trip. After a couple of days in Rome, we headed to Florence and then to the Riviera Di Lavante to explore the Cinque Terre national park. The park's five tiny villages, Riomaggiore, Manorola, Corniglia, Vernazza, and Monterosso, are each nestled in the costal cliffs peering out over the Gulf of Genova and are connected by a series of narrow footpaths running along the walls of the cliffs. This seven-mile trek is one of the most popular in Europe, though many hikers do not make it past a bottle of wine at one of the several cliff-perched cafés. I am happy to report that Dorothy and I did not settle for such a relaxed afternoon. No, we were committed to making things hard on ourselves. It is in our nature to accidentally stumble down the road less traveled. How else would we keep you people entertained?

We boldly struck out to conquer the whole trail. By 11:00 that morning, we were lost somewhere between Manorola and Corniglia. Most of the trails connecting the villages run along the side of the cliff and are relatively flat. Somehow, we made a wrong turn and randomly chose a path which lead over the cliff rather than around it. Well, actually, it wasn't so random. About thirty minutes earlier, Dorothy and I disagreed on which path to take. Turns out, she was right. But as any man knows, there is no admitting that at the time.

"Jeremy, I told you we should have gone that other way. We would be in the next town already. Are we ever going to reach the top of this cliff?"

---

2.   Or what the hell do you call those guys? The gondola skipper? The gondola captain? The gondola pole pusher? I honestly don't know.

Editor's note to author—Gondoliers. (Italian: *gondoliere*).

Author's response to editor—Uh, thanks, I guess.

"Honey, there is supposed to be an incredible view at the top of this cliff. That other path is for old people who are too out of shape to take this trail. They are really missing out. I mean, we could have taken the train between each town if speed was your main concern. I thought you wanted to take a nice invigorating stroll in the great outdoors."

I huffed and puffed up the side of the cliff, burping up carbohydrate exhaust from too much pasta the night before, doing my best to act like I was having fun. After another twenty minutes of near heart-attack inducing exertion, Dorothy started in again. "Jeremy, I think we are lost."

"Babe, we're not lost. We are almost at the top of the cliff. Hey look, there are some more hikers at the top of this ridge. We can ask them."

As we approached the hikers, one of them waved and yelled, "So you guys took the wrong turn as well!"

Dorothy turned to me and smirked. Thanks, buddy. I should have thrown that guy off the cliff. Anyway, the hikers were a group of American college students on a semester abroad. As we rested, we swapped travel stories. By the time Dorothy finished telling them about our around-the-world adventure, they looked at us as if we were travel gods. "You guys must be the most seasoned travelers I know," one of the girls said. "You will have to share all your travel tips."

I just stared at her and thought to myself, "Well, honey, I'm flattered, but I hate to point out that in my vast travel wisdom, I somehow managed to get us lost on one of the best-marked trails in all of Europe." Dorothy, however, shot right back at her with, "The first bit of advice is not to trust your husband with the map."

Ha ha. Anyway, the girls hiked with Dorothy asking questions like, "Where have you met the nicest people?" "Do you feel like you have changed as a person?" and "Do you miss your family and friends back home?" The guy hung back with me and asked more manly travel questions, like "What country has the best-looking women?" and "Where can you find the cheapest beer?"

We finally rejoined the main trail and completed the hike with our new travel buddies. At the final town, we said our goodbyes, and Dorothy and I boarded a train for Venice.

On the train, we sat next to an American family. Or perhaps they were a traveling circus. The two boys were fighting over their McDonald's fries. "Billy took my fries, Dad!" Smack. He landed a good punch on his brother's arm.

"Aaah! Dad, Daniel hit me." Billy dipped a fry in ketchup and launched it at his brother's face.

Dad was trying to rise above the situation by randomly announcing facts from the travel guidebook. He proclaimed each bit of trivia as if fondly recalling it from his personal travel memoirs. "Honey, did you know Venice is built on 117 islands nestled amongst some 150 canals and is connected by approximately 400 bridges?"

"That's nice, dear. Billy, don't take your brother's fries. Daniel, don't hit your brother."

"You little dork! You got ketchup on my shirt." Daniel returned fire with a pickle. It was a clean shot to the forehead.

Dad was undeterred by the group's lack of interest. "Honey, did you know that it was from Venice that Marco Polo set sail for China in 1271?"

"Fascinating, darling. Boys, quit throwing your food."

The daughter spent her train ride making one of those diamond-shaped, folded-paper fortunetellers that you slip over your index fingers and thumbs. "Mom, I want to tell you your fortune. Choose a number."

"Eight."

"One, two, three, four, five, six, seven, eight." She moved her fingers and thumbs back and forth with each count. At eight, she stopped and revealed the colored tabs to her mother. "OK, now choose a color."

"Red."

The girl pealed back the red tab and read her mother's fortune. "You will get sick."

Mom was tickled; Dad was appalled, "How could you even write that as a possible fortune?"

"If I only wrote nice fortunes, then it wouldn't be very honest, would it?"

Mom was even more tickled. Dad was still not pleased, but was happy to use the conversation to share more knowledge. "Well I guess, sweetie. By the way, did you know that Venice lost its main opera house, the Teatro La Fenice, to a fire in 1996?"

"Great, Dad."

The brakes squealed as we pulled into the next station. Billy stood up on his chair and pointed out the window. "Cool. Is this Venice, Dad?"

All passengers within earshot were startled awake and sprung to their feet. Most had already retrieved their overhead bags before Mom called off the charge. "False alarm. Sorry about that, everyone. This is Mestre, an industrial suburb of Venice."

Could you imagine their disappointment if they had stepped off the train? Dad would have lost it. "Mystical and enchanting, my ass. Those gondolas look like normal old barges."

Fifteen minutes later, we were in Venice. Despite the crowds and the cost, Venice is everything it is cracked up to be. Where as Rome is awe-inspiring in its cultural grandeur, Venice is captivating in its romantic timelessness. There are no cars anywhere. There is no modern architecture. With the exception of the occasional ringing mobile phone or hum of a boat motor, it is easy to stroll hand-in-hand through the narrow alleyways along the canals quite convinced you are back in the days of Casanova.

However, you are quickly brought back to 2003 when you ask the cost of a gondola ride. Forty minutes for $80, and rates go up after dark. I almost croaked. I tried to negotiate with the guy, pointing out that I could fly to London for less. He informed me that all gondolas were owned by the same company and that the fares were non-negotiable. The owner of that company must be laughing all the way to the bank. I now plan to expand the Sonnenburgoni brand name into the Venice gondola market. There is a fortune to be made.

Anyway, I have to wrap up. I hear a pizza calling my name. Now, if only I could find my sunglasses. Until next time, arrivederci.

The Fraternal Order of German Beer Drinkers

◆

April 26, 2003
Munich, Germany

"The laws governing German brewing standards have not changed in over 487 years," our waiter proclaimed as he plonked a frothy stein of *dunkles*[1] on the table in front of me. "That is why our beer is the best in the world. Go ahead, try it."

I toasted him with my mug and then tasted the beer as instructed. It was so good I almost wept. I have searched the world over for the perfect beer, and now

---

1. Dark German beer with about the same alcohol content as bourbon—well, almost.

we had found each other. It was a very emotional moment. I took another gulp and then remembered our waiter. "Very tasty indeed. Is this from a local brewery?" I asked.

He was all smiles. "Yes. The beer you are drinking is brewed by monks. The best beer in the world!" He gave me a hearty slap on the back and moved off to help another table.

Monks who brew beer? I have never heard of this before. Let me make sure I understand. We are talking about a group of serious beer drinkers who pledge an oath to live in the same house, call each other brothers, and operate under a cloud of secrecy. Sounds like an American fraternity moved over and set up shop as a monastery, if you ask me. It's actually quite a good idea. They would have no problem recruiting from the masses of American frat boys who backpack through Europe each summer.

"Bring the new pledge before the altar. Kneel and reveal to the High Fraternal Order of German Beer Drinkers why you wish to join their brotherhood."

"Uh, right dude. Well, I thought about it, and like, I don't want to graduate and get a real job. That would, like, really suck. So, I thought I would just pledge your German beer-drinking frat and hang out with you guys."

"The pledge is wise. You will find that not only do we get to hang out and drink good German beer, but we also have several social mixers with the nuns at the local convents."

"Sweet! Sign me up."

"Very well, now onto the pledgeship rituals—strip and put on your gimp mask."

Anyway, that evening Dorothy and I went to Hofbrahaus, a massive Bavarian beer hall. It was good-natured, rowdy drunkenness at its very best. People of all ages were drinking beer out of liter-sized mugs built to withstand the boisterous enthusiasm of the crowd. People swayed back and forth at long wooden tables to horns and drums from the traditional German oompah band. The band only played two or three songs per set because their music quickly cranked up the crowd to a near frenzied state. By about the second song, the music was mere background noise to the clinking of glasses, pounding on tables, and bellowing attempts from the drunken audience to sing along. Ah, it reminded me of my childhood.

Anyway, I'd be lying if I told you this place wasn't a tourist trap. However, the droves of American backpackers don't arrive in Europe until late May, so most of the other tourists in the beer hall were Germans visiting Munich for the weekend. We were immediately adopted by one such group that was cycling through southern Germany. Each time the band cranked up, we all crashed our beer mugs together and started swaying to and fro while singing along. The songs were in German, but it didn't matter. After two or three of those large beers, I could yodel with the best of them.

Yo-da-lay-yo-da-lay-ee-who! Yo-da-lay-yo-da-lay-ee-who!

I can't remember if I was the only one yodeling or if there where others, but the Germans at my table thought I was great. I think. Dorothy just sat there and shook her head. She must have been proud of me. Well, I know one thing for sure—I thought I was great and I was proud of me.

The highlight of the night was a Bavarian rendition of "Take Me Home Country Road." I had no idea John Denver had such a German following, but the crowd went crazy. People stood on the tables singing arm-in-arm with such passion that it seemed like the song was about the German heartland. And they sang it in English.

> Country road, take me home
> To the place I belong
> West Virginia, mountain mama
> Take me home, country roads
> Yo-da-lay-yo-da-lay-ee-who!

Even the Germans around us who didn't speak English knew every word to that song. I point this out because it could be very useful when trying to communicate with cab drivers in Germany. Just make sure to limit your English vocabulary to the lyrics of "Take Me Home Country Road." Hop in the back seat, hand the driver your hotel address, and then in your best country-folk voice, sing "Take me home to the place I belong." I would imagine this works especially well if you are staying in a place called the West Virginia Inn on a street named Country Road; but hey, what are the chances? I wouldn't recommend yodeling at the driver. The more I think about it, the more uncertain I become that anyone in Germany yodels. I am growing increasingly convinced that I was the lone yodeler in the beer hall. Your driver might end up taking you to somewhere like Switzerland or Austria—or maybe Texas if he was in Hofbrahaus last night.

But back to "Take Me Home Country Road." How do you think an American folk song became so popular in a German beer hall? I spent all day thinking about this. I decided it has to be the influence of the frat-daddy monks who brew the beer.

The Multilingual Matador

✦

May 1, 2003
Barcelona, Spain

Our plane touched down in Barcelona, Spain, a couple of days ago. As we disembarked the aircraft, one of the flight attendants bid me farewell, "Adios señor. Que tenga un buen dia."

Ahhhhhh! It was the Ghost of Spanish Past! How appropriate that I would spend the final week of the trip haunted by the same foreign language that eluded me during our first three months of travel. I tried to bluff her with a pleasant smile. She didn't buy it. "Have a good day, sir," she translated. She must have seen the confused-or-possibly-constipated expression I give when trying to remember long-forgotten Spanish phrases.

We proceeded to baggage collection and then hailed a cab. Dorothy was in full Spanish mode in no time at all, giving the cab driver directions to the hotel, asking about Barcelona, and telling him all about our travels. During a lull in the conversation, she gave my arm a little squeeze and said, "Oh, isn't it great we get to practice our Spanish again."

No. "Ah, yeah. Sure, honey."

Once we got to the hotel, Dorothy left me in line to check in as she went in search of a Diet Coke. As I feared, she had not returned by the time it was my turn. I had anticipated this possibility and mentally prepared my Spanish phrase while waiting in line. I let it rip: "Buenas tardes. Yo tengo una reservacion. Mi apellido es Sonnenburg." *(Good afternoon. I have a reservation. My last name is Sonnenburg.)*

Uh oh. He knew I was a fake. I could see it in his eyes. This guy could probably speak six different languages and there was no way he was about to let me convince myself, or anyone else in that hotel lobby, that I could speak anything other than lazy-ass-American English. It was now his obligation to slaughter my Spanish before the blood-thirsty crowd of native speakers. He stepped forward into the arena. He was the multilingual matador; I was the tongue-tied *toro*. He paused as the trumpets blared, gave a slight nod to the Spaniards behind me and then launched into his response. His eyes narrowed into a focused stare as his tongue gained momentum. When his torrent concluded, the Spaniards cheered, "Ole!"

I tried to stay cool, thinking if I showed a little humility, he would spare me. "No entiendo. Repita mas despacio, por favor." *(I don't understand. Repeat it slower please.)*

More trumpets. He could smell the kill. He erupted into another tirade. He spoke so rapidly that sparks flew from his mouth every time he rolled his R's. When he finished, he stomped his foot and dramatically waved his arm to his Spanish audience. "Ole!"

I decided to beg. Perhaps he would show some mercy. "Señor, no entiendo. Es posible para usted repita un poco mas despacio, por favor?" *(Sir, I don't understand. Is it possible for you to repeat it a little bit slower, please?)*

More trumpets. The Spaniards were chanting. They wanted him to finish me off. He clicked his heels and burst into the climax. The crowd roared. He continued for two minutes, then three, then four. He was working himself into a frenzy.

What on earth was this guy ranting about? Was he quoting Don Quixote from memory? Where was freakin' Dorothy when I needed her?

"I GIVE UP! I am a fraud. I don't speak Spanish. Please spare me and switch to English!!!"

"Ole! Ole! Bravo!" The Spaniards showered him with flowers. He smiled in a smug, bilingual sort of way and said, "Welcome to the hotel. Your room is now ready."

More trumpets. More cheering. More flowers. The crowds waved flags as the president of the hotel presented him a trophy. Finally, Dorothy returned with her Diet Coke and we retreated to our hotel room. After a quick rest to recover my self-composure and staunch the blood flow, we headed off to explore Barcelona.

Barcelona is an eclectic cocktail of art, fashion, food, and late-night fun poured between a couple of hills and the Mediterranean Sea. The city is architecturally defined by Antoni Gaudí's animated colored tiles and wavy, curved walls. Most evenings out end with sunlight on your face. A visit to the city is so surreal that it feels like you are drifting in one long daydream through an artsy-Spanish mirage overlooking the sea.

We spent the next couple of days checking out Barcelona's art scene. We visited a Salvador Dali exhibit, the Picasso Museum, and Antoni Gaudí's La Sagrada Familia and Park Güell. All of these were great, but I was most impressed by all the human statues along La Rambla. If you have never seen a human statue before, it is exactly what it sounds like. Some dude stands real still and pretends he's a statue. And get this—people walk buy and put money in his collection box. They are becoming commonplace in most large cities now, but whoever first came up with the idea is a genius. I can only imagine the street entertainers in the inaugural human statue performance:

"So Billy, what are we going to do today? Juggle? Magic tricks? Spin plates?"

"Man I am really sick of all those circus antics. I was thinking about it last night, and you know what this city needs? A human statue!"

"Billy, are you drunk? What on earth are you talking about?"

"No, no. Get this. I will paint all my clothes silver. I will also paint my face and my arms silver. I will die my hair silver. Everything will be silver! When I stand still, I will look like a statue!"

"Yeah, but Billy, people don't give money to statues."

"That's the point! People are always looking for new ways to give away their money. They want to give money to statues. They just haven't thought about it yet!"

"Well, good luck. I am going to go get the juggling balls. Don't try to borrow money tonight when you are broke."

And human statues took off like wildfire. It started with just a few silver statues in a couple of cities. Then they were everywhere—and everything. In a matter of years I saw white statues, bronzed statues, golden statues, celebrity statues, war veteran statues, Greek gods and goddesses, and many more. The best one I saw was a guy in New Orleans one time. He claimed to be the *drunk bum* statue. He would get liquored up, and then climb up on a box with a can of beer in his hand. He would try his best to stand still, but would inevitable start swaying and fall off. Every time somebody would drop a coin in his box, he would take a drink and pronounce in a drunken slur, "Thanths, I theally neethed that." I stood there and watched him go through a six-pack in ten minutes. Today, that bum is probably some posh millionaire who frequents trendy rehab programs in California.

The street artists in Barcelona have clearly taken human statues to a new level. If you walk along La Rambla, you will see at least twenty human statues, each with his or her own gimmick.

First there was the Paella con Cabeza *(traditional Spanish rice dish with head).*

Every time someone would drop a coin in his bucket, he would open his eyes and scream, "Gracias, señor!"

Then there was Che Guevara.

Every time someone would drop a coin in his bucket, he would puff his cigar and show the peace sign. Now, I admit that I am not a Che Guevara expert, but wasn't he a Latin American communist who advocated militant revolutions to fight the spread of capitalism, imperialism, and globalization? And wasn't he the author of two books on guerilla warfare? If so, I am sure he would appreciate the irony of one of his impersonators standing on the other side of the world on a main tourist street offering the peace sign to people in exchange for money. Oh well, at least this guy has the Cuban cigar right.

Then I came to…wait. Hold on a minute. It was the guy from the hotel reception desk, the multilingual matador.

There was no way I was going to drop money into his bucket. I already knew his gimmick. He would berate me in Spanish. Been there, done that, and I'll pass this time, thanks.

Happy Trails to You

◆

May 3, 2003
35,000 feet over the Atlantic Ocean

Well my friends, our flight is due to land in New York in less than three hours, bringing our little around-the-world adventure to its conclusion. I can't even begin to tell you how much I have grown as a person since we started traveling eight months ago. Well, actually I can. I grew exactly sixteen pounds as a person. I have a theory to explain this growth. I figure all that new, worldly knowledge just wouldn't fit inside the old me, so I swelled. Now that knowledge is packed away quite comfortably around my culturally-expanded waistline. I mention my personal growth because it triggered a good idea I had the other day while reviewing some of our recent travel pictures. Cameras need a fat-face reduction feature. They already have red-eye reduction to prevent me from looking like a demonically-possessed, nocturnal beast. How hard could it be to add fat-face reduction to prevent me from looking like a slightly tanned Pillsbury Dough Boy? It would be great! "OK, everybody smile on three. One, two—"

"Hold it, honey. You do have the fat-face reduction turned on, right? Make sure you have enabled the double-chin diminisher, the chiseled-jaw-line enhancer, and the cheek-chub reducer. OK, now we're ready."

Anyway, I will burn off my love handles in the gym when we get home. As for the pictures, well, I guess I will just have to explain those away as Dorothy's experimentation with a new wide-angle lens.

As I looked through the pictures, it was fun to reflect back on the good times we've had on this trip. And with those experiences came some hard-earned lessons. I thought it would be fun to close with a quick review:

Costa Rica

- If you decide to learn to surf in the stingray-infested beaches near Dominical, wear steel-spiked sports cleats. This way you will at least have the satisfaction of drawing first blood.

- If you attempt to learn Spanish in Monteverde, do not try to speak Spanish to your host family, regardless of what your professor advises to the contrary. And make sure you carry a motorcycle helmet with you at all times.

- If you visit San Juan, bring some duct tape so you can strap your valuables to body. Otherwise, go white-water rafting and remember to take a small outboard motor with you.

Peru

- If you visit Cuzco, take canisters of oxygen. You can either use them yourself or sell them for hundreds of dollars to other altitude-afflicted travelers.

- If you hike the Inka Trail, DO NOT CARRY A BIG BACKPACK. Try to hire a porter to carry you and your pack if possible. Be wary of talking to sweet old ladies who have trained rigorously for the hike.

Chile

- If you find yourself craving a Big Mac, you can find one in Arica. Walk up to the nice man at the counter and say, "Numero uno, super-sized, por favor."

- If you visit San Pedro de Atacama and stumble across a horse named Frank, please shoot him for me.

Brazil

- If you travel to Rio, use your Marriott points to stay at their hotel on Copacabana Beach. Tell them you know me. They will either upgrade you to a suite or ask you to leave. I am not sure which.

Argentina

- If you go hiking in Patagonia, make sure that you remember to pack a lunch or are prepared to eat your guide—just make sure there is somebody left who can hoist you up the ice wall.

- If you plan to go trout fishing in Ushuuaia, practice casting before you go. Actually, who am I kidding? Just go order the trout in the restaurant and forget the fishing.

New Zealand

- If you fly into Auckland on a flight that takes two days, do not attempt to drive a camper van the day you land. Don't forget to go caving and contemplate the glowing worm shit.

- If you go wine tasting in New Zealand, smell the wine and tell them you can make out slight hints of doozleberry. The others on the tour will think you are a wine connoisseur. Also, arm yourself in advance with a few funny comments to write in the guest book.

Australia

- If you decide to climb Sydney Harbor Bridge, don't have anything to drink earlier that day. Also, you might see a group of strapping Aussie blokes trying to carry a shopping cart full of beer up to the arch of the bridge. If so, offer to give them a hand. They would do the same for you.

- If you go to Byron Bay, it is essential that you show up with a tan. When you go to the beach, wear dark sunglasses and bring your camera. When you go out for the evenings, bring a set of bras and panties in your pocket. It might be good for free pitcher of beer.

- If you go on the self-drive tour to Fraser Island, allow yourself more than 5 minutes to do your grocery shopping. Also, be patient. Remember that bad things happen in sets of three. The evening campfires on the beach will more than make up for the frustrations of off-road driving. And it is important to pick a tough name for your group. Be advised though—the Mighty Smurfs has already been claimed.

- If you ever play a Brit at Scrabble, remember that 'knave' and 'queen' might be more high-browed, but 'farts' could get you more points. Let the Brits show good form in their game, but any flag-waving American should play to win.

- If you go camping in Kakadu National Park, take a fly net, don't swim in any croc-infested water, and watch out for the ferocious frill lizard.

- If you visit Perth, check the weather before opting to stay in a hostel with no air-conditioning. A ceiling fan isn't going to save you in the middle of a heat wave.

Singapore

- If you stay in a hotel in Singapore, leave a flashlight on the nightstand. Otherwise, you could accidentally bomb China when you go the bathroom in the middle of the night.

Thailand

- If you visit Bangkok and wish to sample the local cuisine, steer clear of the fire sauce. Otherwise, be ready for the pain to follow.

- If you go SCUBA diving in Ao Nang, be forewarned that you will encounter European men running around in bikinis. Also, wear a kilt to the next wedding you attend. You will be a hit with the ladies. Always go commando style.

- If you try windsurfing in Phuket, try to sail parallel to the beach rather than away from it. Also, bring a video camera. Maybe you can catch the Thai flower ninjas in action.

Japan

- If you visit Tokyo, bring a suitcase full of money. Also, try to avoid the Tokyo subways during rush hour, unless you enjoy having a large, gloved man push your head into another commuter's armpit. Check out the Ninja restaurant, but if your traveling on a budget, *fuggedaboudit.*

- If you want to feel like a celebrity, head to Tokyo Disneyland. Maybe by then, Dorothy and I will have returned as Gaijin Gretchen and White-guy Willy. If so, come and visit us in Racially-Integrated Island, where you won't have to worry about those damn fast-pass lines.

- If you want to see Japan at its finest, head to Kyoto during cherry blossom season. For a traditional Japanese experience, stay in a *ryokan*, but be on the lookout for young girls in the men's showers. Have your pictures taken as you and your buddy spar with samurai swords, and then try to lift the wishing stone. Strong, strapping Texan men shouldn't have much of a problem.

- If you are flying to Italy from Japan, watch out for Mary. She is a real stinker.

Italy

- If you want to chow down on Italian food and still look good in the latest Italian fashion, I got you covered: Sonnenburgoni, ghetto-fly garb for the carb lovin' mobster.

Germany

- If you visit Munich, learn the words to "Take Me Home Country Road" and then go drink beer at Hofbrahaus. Refrain from yodeling. I am still not quite sure what got into me.

Spain

- If you are in Barcelona, be on the lookout for the multilingual matador. Don't engage him in conversation unless you have Dorothy with you. Also, if cash is a problem, go buy a few beers and pretend to be the drunk bum human statue on La Rambla. You should make out just fine.

Well, the captain just came on the PA and announced that we should prepare for landing. Happy trails to you, and until we meet again, *pura vida.*

Jeremy

About the Author

Jeremy Sonnenburg grew up in Pasadena, Texas, then home to the world-famous Gilley's Honky Tonk (see Urban Cowboy). Many claim his wacky sense of humor developed after being tossed off the mechanical bull and landing on his head. After traveling with him, his wife, Dorothy, tends to agree.

0-595-28182-6